How Smart Small Businesses Grow

The Five Keys To Marketing

Elaine Schneider

AuthorHouse™
1663 Liberty Drive, Suite 200
Bloomington, IN 47403
www.authorhouse.com
Phone: 1-800-839-8640

© 2007 Elaine Schneider. All rights reserved.

No part of this book may be reproduced, stored in a retrieval system, or transmitted by any means without the written permission of the author.

First published by AuthorHouse 8/15/2007

ISBN: 978-1-4343-0606-7 (sc)

Printed in the United States of America
Bloomington, Indiana

This book is printed on acid-free paper.

INTRODUCTION

Small-business owners tend to lump sales and marketing together. As a result, they don't create the marketing infrastructure they need to grow the business, and their business gets stuck.

My five-step formula for creating a marketing infrastructure takes the guesswork out of marketing. I arrived at the formula by observing three things: the common patterns that keep small companies from growing, the methods successful companies use to structure their businesses, and the steps I took to help unsuccessful companies get back on track.

My five-step formula for creating a marketing infrastructure creates the "flywheel effect" your business needs to attract more customers, create compelling products and services, and develop the kind of credibility that makes the selling process effortless. I promise it will have a higher payback and cost less than shotgun sales and marketing initiatives. Sound exciting? Actually it is. Nitty-gritty marketing may not be glamorous, but watching your business skyrocket can be exciting.

LANGUAGE

I like the word *customer* rather than client, member, or patient. Terms like client and patient have connotations that don't suggest power and therefore create the wrong orientations in an organization.

I also use the term *product* when talking about a service or product. It is essential to make services tangible. For instance, a self-service car wash is a service. An automated car wash is also a service, but you can "productize" it by offering packages. For instance, a "Super Wash Package" may include things like vacuuming the interior, polishing the hubcaps, and sealing the underside.

How To Use This Book

I included some exercises at the end of some of the chapters. You may also want to encourage other members of your organization to read the book. In talking to executives I learned that leading book discussions with their teams turned out to be some of the best experiences of their careers.

Contents

Introductory Remarks — v

Part One: The Case For A Marketing Infrastructure — 1

Chapter 1	What's Marketing Got To Do With It?	3
Chapter 2	Marketing And Selling Are Codependent	8
Chapter 3	Marketing Infrastructure Basics	13
Chapter 4	The Marketing Infrastructure Advantage	20
Chapter 5	Sales-Driven vs. Marketing-Driven	27

Part Two: Initiating Action — 35

Chapter 6	Mapping Out A Path Forward	37
Chapter 7	Talking To Customers And Prospects	45
Chapter 8	Creating Superior Lead Systems	53
Chapter 9	Rethinking Your Market	62
Chapter 10	Growing Beyond One Market	70
Chapter 11	Positioning Your Product	76
Chapter 12	Developing New Products	87
Chapter 13	Industry Influencers and Public Relations	94
Chapter 14	Working With Reporters	107
Chapter 15	Execution	115

Part Three: Creating The Right Launching Pad — 121

Chapter 16	Why Small Businesses Self-Destruct	123
Chapter 17	Getting Everyone On The Same Page	128
Chapter 18	Selling – The Ultimate Test Of Execution	134
Chapter 19	The Care And Feeding Of Customers	145
Chapter 20	New Trends In Marketing	155
Chapter 21	Answers To Special Challenges	165
Chapter 22	Finding The Right Marketing Resources	174
Chapter 23	Creating The Results You Want	181

Reference Notes — 188

Appendix: A Guide To Event Planning — 192

About the Author — 207

PART ONE

THE CASE FOR A MARKETING INFRASTRUCTURE (CHAPTERS 1-5)

Part One makes a compelling case for a marketing infrastructure. A marketing infrastructure consists of five elements: strategy, dialogues with customers, market or niche focus, relationships with Industry Influencers, and execution. The five dimensions of a marketing infrastructure are also the five keys to marketing your business.

This section begins by showing the limitations of thinking of marketing as simply sales and promotion. To appreciate the advantages of a marketing infrastructure, you may want to quickly review the detailed list under the heading "Key Results Of A Marketing Infrastructure" in Chapter 4.

A marketing infrastructure is an essential component of creating the foundation for growth. Without a marketing infrastructure, organizations cycle between boom and bust—between getting traction and going back to the drawing board.

As this book will show, organizations with a marketing infrastructure generate more business from existing customers, get rid of what's not working, and create better and more profitable products.

Chapter 1

What's Marketing Got To Do With It?

Lots of small-business owners lump sales and marketing together. This is a mistake of the highest order. Marketing is a broad umbrella; sales is just one very critical dimension. If done right, a marketing infrastructure will create a flywheel effect that generates more profitable business and leads to products that solve the limitations of the status quo.

The usual sign that an organization needs to create a marketing infrastructure is that every few months everything stops while the business focuses on generating leads in the pipeline.

Why Hiring A Salesperson Won't Work

To solve this problem, the first instinct of a small-business owner is to hire a salesperson to generate more sales at the top of the sales funnel. This will not work without a marketing infrastructure.

The reason is simple. A marketing infrastructure creates the credibility necessary to overcome resistance from more conservative buyers (the ones you'll run into as the business matures).

Consider this: in the early stages of a business, the key people in the business utilize their personal contacts and in-depth industry knowledge to sell to people who are predisposed to their solution (including, perhaps, the organization they left to start their own business).

As the small-business owner looks for ways to generate more business, it seems logical to him or her to find other people who can accomplish the same objective. Unfortunately, it is rare to find someone who embodies the three things the owner usually has—namely credibility, contacts, and in-depth product knowledge.

Furthermore, without a marketing infrastructure, the new salesperson is forced to use direct promotional tactics in order to sell. This puts the salesperson at a distinct disadvantage, particularly if the organization is working in many markets.

Unless the salesperson has a title commensurate with the C-level executive who has the most influence over the decision, it will be difficult to gain access during the sales process. This senior-level executive will also "carry the day" in terms of defining the problem or improvement issue and consequently in determining the quality of the solution.

To make the case for a marketing infrastructure, let's examine some all-too-common scenarios that suggest ways the organization has failed to move beyond its roots in sales. Here are three common scenarios that play out every day in business:

Scenario 1

A small consulting business wants to grow the business. The two principals hire a business development manager to beat the bushes for new business. After about six months, they fire the salesperson. Here are some of the reasons this happened:

1. The two principals resist providing access to their past customers. The business development manager must develop leads in a vacuum.

2. The business development manager has a background in one of the three areas of the business, but is not familiar with the other specialty areas.

3. The consulting firm works in eight markets. The business development manager is familiar with a few of their success stories, but no scripts or testimonials are available.

4. The nature of the consulting practice requires access to C-level decision makers. The business development manager does not have the credibility or title necessary to gain access to the CEO and other C-level executives.

SCENARIO 2

The owner of a successful consulting firm wants to hire three or four salespeople to promote a new product that is incongruent with the key services the firm has offered in the past. Because there is concern about the viability of this new product, the salespeople are pushing hard to find customers.

Ironically, the new consulting product is intended to help organizations with internal branding issues (something my client also appears to need help with since their new product is inconsistent with their brand, and no one in the organization has any marketing, much less internal branding, experience).

I ask the owner if she has done any phone surveys with customers to gauge their level of interest in the new product. She has not. Gradually she begins to see why it might make sense to talk to customers. Customer conversations would enable her organization to match customers' current challenges with one or more of the services her organization provides. In this way, she could estimate the amount of revenue the firm might expect from current products (which constitute the mainstay of the business) while also setting up sales opportunities for the new product.

These conversations share a common pattern in small businesses looking to create more consistent streams of revenue. The common pattern is:

1. They don't develop new business from the customer base.

2. Little effort is put into what the customers are thinking.

3. They don't let salespeople have access to their existing customers, but rather focus them on new prospects.

4. New products are created without any feedback from the customer.

5. They engage in magical thinking by believing "feet on the street" will solve the problem.

Scenario 3

A consulting firm is losing traction in the market. Like a lot of businesses, the firm is in six different markets and has not developed a dialogue with customers. For all of the above reasons, the firm cannot link its practice to a key problem in the customers' organizations. The firm's competitors can. This results in the following consequences:

1. The firm is in so many markets it can't speak the language of its customers.

2. It doesn't have an effective way of getting the attention of C-level buyers.

3. Its solutions and approach are dated.

4. Because it is not solving a key problem, the firm does not have a relationship with its customers.

THE MISSING PIECE

The missing element in all of these scenarios is marketing. Early in the business, it is critical to create a marketing infrastructure. To review:

> *A marketing infrastructure embodies the five keys to marketing your business. It consists of five elements: strategy, customer dialogues, market or niche focus, relationships with Industry Influencers, and execution.*

A marketing infrastructure allows the business to leverage existing customer relationships (to create more business) and create a single market segment it can dominate.

Chapter 2

Marketing And Selling Are Codependent

In a nutshell, here is the relationship between sales and marketing. Once you understand your customer (marketing), you are able to create products that sell. As a result, you are able to sell to more people because your inventory consists of products that customers and prospects want (sales).

> *Peter Drucker said the same thing when he observed that "The aim of marketing is to understand your customers so well the product sells itself." [1]*

But there is another important dynamic between sales and marketing. Marketing activities can also generate money. For example, any time I conduct a phone survey, I can expect to find at least five pieces of new business per twenty-seven respondents (Of course, I'm selective about whom I contact).

What Exactly Is Marketing?

In *The Invisible Touch* Harry Beckwith says, "Marketing is the brains of the business."[2] Marketing touches every aspect of a business: how well customer service solves problems, how well your organization positions itself, how well the organization executes, and everything else.

Because everyone has a different concept of what marketing is, it's a good idea to create a visual of the marketing process before engaging in group decision making regarding the allocation of marketing resources (or any other marketing-related discussion).

In teaching marketing to working professionals, I found the simplest way to do this is to create a mental model of how all the key marketing activities relate. The key marketing activities include strategy, product development, marketing communications, pricing, execution, and audit.

For instance, if you are doing a direct marketing campaign, you will need to consider marketing communications (brochure, business reply card, Internet, etc.), pricing, execution (telemarketing, etc.), and audit (how you will measure results).

It also introduces some rigor to the marketing process. I've noticed that even in marketing-challenged businesses, everyone is perfectly comfortable providing marketing advice.

IMPLICATIONS FOR YOUR BUSINESS

We need to boil down what we have learned so far. Let's start with a basic definition.

> *Marketing is the art and science of maximizing the organization's capacity to provide the highest possible (and most profitable) value exchange between the organization and its stakeholders.*

To do this, you must find new ways to differentiate your product every day, and you need to create systems, processes, and tools that will lead to a consistent flow of profitable business.

You can't get to the point where your product sells itself without spending a lot of time talking to customers and prospective customers. This is the linchpin of creating a marketing infrastructure.

It is also why the strategy of hiring a salesperson to go out and beat the bushes for business rarely works. They need to be part of building a focused marketing effort that starts with creating a marketing infrastructure.

In his book *Relationship Marketing*, Regis McKenna says, "To build lasting positions in the market companies must first build strong relationships with customers, suppliers, distributors, resellers, Industry Influencers and members of the financial community."[3]

This requires creating a dialogue between the company and the customer and between the company and the market. It differs from traditional approaches that consist of superficial promotional strategies involving one-way communication (often without the benefit of qualifying the customer or asking his or her permission).

Your sales team also needs the benefit of referrals from your customers; otherwise you'll be like one of my small business clients who could have gotten about $500 thousand in immediate new business from his current customers but instead hired a salesperson to develop a new territory that lacked even a rudimentary lead system. If you want a salesperson to be successful, you can't be territorial about your customer base.

WHY MARKETING HAS A BAD RAP

Marketing impacts every aspect of the business and yet it is perceived by many as a costly activity of questionable value. Here are three reasons this is often true:

1. Many marketers are specialists. A marketing communications expert may be excellent in the design of marketing materials, but may not be qualified to help an organization develop a strategy.

2. Many marketers disavow any relationship to the sales process. If you are going to hire a marketing consultant, you need someone

who will generate more business in the process of executing the marketing job at hand.

3. Traditional promotional strategies are dead. Advertising and direct mail rarely work unless they are embedded into a larger promotion, such as an annual customer conference. Here are some reasons why:
    - The average person screens out almost three thousand advertising messages per day.
    - It's a buyers' market. A global economy offers a limitless number of options.
    - Prospective customers want a dialogue, not a monologue.
    - Customers and prospects want personalized messages. A glitzy direct marketing piece rarely works; a personalized e-mail often does.

THE RATIONALE FOR A MARKETING INFRASTRUCTURE

If traditional marketing tactics no longer work, what does? The key is to start with a foundation, much like one does when building a house.

A marketing infrastructure enables you to create a superior lead system, foster deep relationships with customers and prospective customers, and develop more profitable business by becoming an expert in an industry.

> *Once you've created a marketing infrastructure, you are in a position to consider hiring additional salespeople, and you will find that the selling process is collaborative rather than a tug-of-war between you and the buyer.*

CHAPTER 2

END-OF-THE-CHAPTER QUESTIONS

1. What big questions about your customer do you wish you understood better?

2. Name one key pain of your customers.

Chapter 3

Marketing Infrastructure Basics

Many small businesses reach the breaking point when they realize that every few months they find themselves trying to fill the top of the sales funnel. This usually indicates a lack of a marketing infrastructure.

The First Step

Fortunately most small companies can make the transition to a marketing infrastructure with a minimal investment of money. The first step is to identify whether you are missing critical customer data. If you are, someone in the organization may be able to conduct a brief phone survey, or you may find a small consulting firm that can conduct the research for you (Later chapters will include details on how to do this).

The second issue is strategic. If you are currently in six to eight markets, you need to figure out which market is the best fit. This will require an ongoing dialogue with the key people in your organization (or if you operate alone, some careful thought).

It's a good idea to schedule a specific time each week to consider these key questions. The timeframe can be as short as two hours. Over time you will see progress (In subsequent chapters we will explore how other small firms made the transition).

SOME BUSINESSES ARE SUCCESSFUL IN MANY MARKETS

It's true that some businesses develop highly specialized products that can be used by a wide range of businesses or consumers. If you look closely, however, you will find that the business must spend a disproportionate amount of time on promotion.

Part of the problem is that they are in too many markets to keep tabs on where C-level executives convene. In contrast, a business that specializes in one market segment will be using its time to make presentations to audiences of C-level executives.

> *If a disproportionate amount of the organization's time is spent on direct marketing activities, the lack of meaningful customer interactions will make it more difficult to adjust their product to the changing needs of their customers.*

DEVELOPING AN ONGOING STREAM OF REVENUE

In order to leverage the value of a marketing infrastructure, your goal should be to create an ongoing stream of revenue from every customer. The best way to do that is to create a subscription service. A simple example is a public relations consultant providing a set of services on monthly retainer.

Let's look at what happens without a subscription model. ABC sells manufacturing equipment. The company's services involve consulting, training, and installation. Once the equipment has been installed, the company must find another customer.

XYZ provides a decision support system that enables organizations to manage employee health-care costs. Instead of selling the software system to a customer, the company provides a set of deliverables that includes training, consulting, and (this is the key) monthly database updates for a fixed price each year.

How can this approach be justified to the customer? It's simple. The nature of the data is complex. The customer requires assistance in interpreting the data.

Any situation requiring the organization to "compensate" lends itself to a subscription service. If what is needed is not needed consistently or the resources are hard to find or the seller can do it better or cheaper, a subscription service has value.

If the seller can deliver what they promise, they can renew the contract each year. It also enables them to sell other products. Sales approaches for accomplishing this objective include:

1. Cross selling: Selling related products.

2. Up-selling: Recommending enhanced products or services.

3. Maintenance: Including maintenance contracts which may involve regular upgrades.

4. Customized solution: Developing a superior product solution.

The Five Elements of A Marketing Infrastructure

To review, in order to create a sustainable business, you need to create a marketing infrastructure. This involves five key activities: strategy, customer dialogues, market or niche focus, relationships with Industry Influencers, and execution. These five activities are also the five keys to marketing. Here is a brief rundown of each element of a marketing infrastructure:

Strategy

In the short run, strategy is about capitalizing on your unique strengths. In the long run, strategy centers on figuring out what you can do better than anyone else.

In the book *Your Life As Art*, Robert Fritz says, "A good strategy often begins with easier steps that can generate a quick start, followed by more involved steps that deepen and broaden the project, followed by more complex steps that enable us to do those things that would have been highly unlikely or even impossible before the earlier steps were taken." [4]

> You can back into a "killer strategy" when you create a marketing infrastructure. Dialogues with customers create the opportunity to uncover what your organization can do better than anyone else (In subsequent chapters you'll see how this is accomplished).

CUSTOMER DIALOGUES

One of the key purposes of a marketing infrastructure is to develop an intelligent plan for managing the care and feeding of customers. Without a robust marketing infrastructure, organizations get so distracted by internal product or service delivery concerns that customers become second fiddle.

The research on why customers leave shows that a significant number leave because they do not feel like the organization cares about whether or not they remain a customer. Because it's been known for over thirty years that it costs at least five times as much to acquire a new customer, you might think organizations would create incentives for keeping customers. Sadly, this is often not the case. Many businesses fail to design policies that lead to effective customer relationships.

Most CEOs I've talked to readily admit they don't know the key business pains of their customers. To their credit, they recognize that it's a problem; however, they don't proactively create a system for talking to customers.

I believe there are three key reasons for this: lack of time and resources, fear of what they will find out, and the natural tendency to take customers for granted (more about this later).

Engaging the customer is the most elemental requirement of growing a business and developing a marketing infrastructure. In fact, many organizations have succeeded despite themselves by developing a dialogue with their customers (In later chapters, we will talk about compensation strategies if you have just a few customers).

Market Or Niche Focus

The most provocative dimension of creating a marketing infrastructure is the notion that a small business needs to focus on one market or niche. Just to be clear, an example of a market segment is the hospital market, which can include hospital systems, hospital alliances, specialized hospitals, regional hospitals, and stand alone hospital facilities. A niche, of course, is more specialized. An example of a niche is university-based hospitals.

Being able to speak knowledgeably about the unique issues of an industry is a key advantage that a marketing infrastructure creates. The natural evolution of all products moves toward greater sophistication.

> *This means that, over time, you must create products with more product attributes in order to continue to provide a meaningful value exchange with customers.*

A focused marketing strategy enables you to do the following things:

1. Know the customer's business as well as, or better than, they do.

2. Develop superior products to address the unique needs of an industry.

3. Create a powerful word-of-mouth referral base.

4. Have a center-stage position in the market.

Relationships With Industry Influencers

Industry Influencers consist of reporters, editors, industry analysts, consultants, and association executives. Creating relationships with Industry Influencers sounds like public relations, but it doesn't have to be.

Small businesses that excel in sales can still be players. If your strength is selling, giving speeches to a key association in your niche can achieve the same results as the best public-relations campaign—namely credibility, visibility, and word-of-mouth referrals.

In some industries, such as software, Industry Influencers are critical to product acceptance. Decision makers rely on Industry Influencers to evaluate various products. Buying decisions are based heavily on their review.

No matter what industry you are in, getting press can also help your customers make the case for you internally. For this reason, it is critical that you send speeches, quotes, and other favorable press to your customers. Of course, you also want to compile a press kit of favorable articles as an introduction when calling on new accounts.

EXECUTION

Execution involves any activity that is intended to generate more business. This includes things like direct marketing campaigns, sales, and sales management (In a later chapter we will discuss examples of good and bad execution).

It's important to remember that solid execution can overcome a weak strategy. In his groundbreaking book *The Marketing Edge*, Thomas Bonoma showed businesses that did a good job on execution trumped businesses with superior strategies.[5]

We can all probably think of organizations that don't have a unique strategy but do have solid execution. Let me give you a simple example.

A local shoe repair shop can work wonders on an old pair of shoes, but it needs more customers. Because it is situated in a busy intersection, a decision is made to entice more customers by putting up a huge yellow banner on the front of the store. It says:

Shoe Shine $2 Boot Shine $3

As new customers come in for a shine, the owner is able to educate them on all the ways in which they can transform their old shoes.

Nothing in the business has changed, but this simple execution tactic enables the business to offer customers a way to turn comfortable, old shoes into "new" shoes for a fraction of the price of a new pair. Six months after implementing this, customers are regularly lined up at the door.

CHAPTER 4

THE MARKETING INFRASTRUCTURE ADVANTAGE

This chapter will make the case for a marketing infrastructure. It will spell out the key results you will reap from each of the five elements of a marketing infrastructure. You will then see why the five dimensions of a marketing infrastructure are also the five keys to marketing your business.

Let's start with a story. A professional services firm is completely out of touch with its customers (and generates zero profit). I agree to spend twenty hours a week conducting phone research.

During each week, we meet to discuss what I've learned. Our key objectives are to improve the value proposition (deliverables) by retooling our products, finding one market segment we can dominate, and using that segment to create a superior lead system. In other words, we want to fill in the missing pieces of a marketing infrastructure.

MISSION ACCOMPLISHED

We are able to accomplish all of those objectives by creating a dialogue with customers. The phone survey also becomes a vehicle for developing more business.

When you develop an ongoing dialogue with customers, you will begin to fill in information in each of the six areas identified in the next section. If an organization continues to talk to customers, decisions are no longer made in a vacuum (and their instincts will be correct almost 100 percent of the time).

KEY RESULTS OF A MARKETING INFRASTRUCTURE

Here are some of the key outcomes you will reap from having an effective marketing infrastructure. It is not intended to be a comprehensive list; the purpose is to show the value of creating a marketing infrastructure.

VALUE OF STRATEGY

Focus
Clarity

VALUE OF CUSTOMER DIALOGUES

Referrals
A superior lead system
Basis for a market or niche strategy
Knowledge of what makes you tick
Success stories
Knowledge of how your product is actually used
Knowledge of what is problematic about your product
Business requirements of each 'Buying Influence' *
How the 'User Buyer' actually uses your product * [6]
Insight into the personality of your customers
Which employees are most effective with customers
Source of funding for new service concepts
Impact of customers' customers
Why a customer selected a competitor

Note: Buying Influence and User Buyer are roles in purchase decisions. The User Buyer manages the implementation of a new product purchase.

Value Of Other Stakeholders (Suppliers/ Distribution Channels, etc.)

Sources of new product ideas
Sources of improvement
Sources of other business

Market Segment Insights

Best market segment (or niche)
Related markets (cruise lines/facility management)
Pains of market segment (or niche)
Creation of industry or niche-specific products
Ways products can be embedded

Value Of Industry Influencers

Credibility
Visibility
Referrals

Execution (based on synthesis from all sources)

Value Proposition
Identity
Unique strengths
Positioning and Brand promise
Linkage between your product and customers' pains

Customer Dialogues Are The Glue

As you can see from all the information collected, a marketing infrastructure leads to more business, profitable niches, and new products. A marketing infrastructure also serves as a decision support system that leads to right actions.

WHAT IF YOU DON'T HAVE MANY CUSTOMERS?

Developing a dialogue with customers is the most critical aspect of the marketing infrastructure, but what if you don't have many customers? We will cover this issue in more detail in the chapter entitled "Answers To Special Challenges." But here is a quick overview of some of the things you can do:

1. View past customers as customers (In other words, find ways to create a dialogue).

2. Reflect back on each customer experience to get new insights into your value.

3. Identify at least one thing customers wanted that you couldn't offer.

4. Conduct a survey of prospects that fit the profile of your ideal customer.

5. Participate in events in your market.

6. Host an executive briefing or focus group.

Elaine Schneider

The Relationship Between Elements Of A Marketing Infrastructure

This shows both the process and the relationship between all the elements of a marketing infrastructure.

Customer Dialogues
Dialogues are the linchpin of creating a marketing infrastructure.

Niche Market
Customer conversations uncover a match between the requirements of a niche market and the seller's unique competencies.

Strategy
Strategy is based on the match between a niche market's requirements and the seller's unique competencies. It indicates what the seller can do better than anyone else.

Industry Influencers
Identification of a niche market leads to the creation of a superior platform for getting noticed by Industry Influencers (big fish in a small pond).

Execution
Execution tactics are based on the interplay of the first four elements. For instance, customer dialogues lead to additional business and identifying a new niche market leads to new business opportunties.

Marketing Without An Infrastructure

Recently I met with five directors of marketing who represented the largest law firms in a region. They told me they believed the key to client retention was superior service. A few days later, a newly appointed managing partner at a leading law firm in Ohio announced that he was going to increase market share by instituting a rigorous Quality program.

This kind of thinking lacks any rigor. Customer satisfaction is the price of entry; it is never the source of differentiation. A customer is satisfied until someone else comes along with a better plan. Winning with Quality is an equally problematic way to distinguish a firm in a crowded market. Unlike manufacturing (where problems can be corrected as the product is built), individuals who work in the service sector have lots of discretion in terms of how a given activity is completed.

More significantly, businesspeople and lawyers usually have different concepts of Quality. This means you cannot create customer satisfaction and improve Quality until you understand what clients value. Beyond that, differentiation comes from a true understanding of an industry and its unique problems.

The fundamental question is, what do clients want from a law firm? Because none of the firms have initiated dialogues with their clients, they can't answer that question. A business that is out of touch with customers cannot improve its market share because it has little insight into true needs.

Chapter 4

End-Of-The-Chapter Questions

1. Based on what you've read so far (and your own experience), how does a marketing infrastructure make your business easier to run?

Chapter 5

Sales-Driven vs. Marketing-Driven

A sales-driven business focuses on telling. It uses tactics such as brochures, telemarketing, and appointment-setting. A marketing-driven business is about engaging.

> *A marketing-driven business seeks first to understand rather than to be understood. It offers up something of value before asking the customer for something.*

It is more difficult to create a marketing-driven approach if you have not adopted a marketing infrastructure. You can only offer up something of value if your organization understands the way in which your product will impact your customer's business as well as or better than your customer does (that's hard to do if you're a small business in four or five unrelated markets). More importantly, you are not positioned in the mind of the customer to offer the most credible solution.

Why Marketing-Driven Is Better

In a sales-driven business, the first step is to meet with a prospect or customer in order to sell something. Because it is direct, it is perceived as being self-serving. As a result, many potential customers tune out even if they have an interest (think of how many times you say no to a telemarketer even when you are intrigued with his or her offer).

In a marketing-driven business, the first step is to offer something of value before you try to sell something. For example, you may host an executive briefing that examines a key challenge in your customers' industry. The point is that it is not a product pitch. You are offering something of value—something without strings.

A marketing-driven approach (if done correctly) is about engaging customers, Industry Influencers and other key stakeholders. It is collaborative by nature, and it tends to draw out customers.

There is nothing wrong with personal selling; it is the key to creating a business. But if you want the business to grow, you must move to a marketing-driven approach. This is because customer dialogues (as opposed to sales dialogues) are the linchpin of creating a marketing infrastructure.

Key Elements of a Marketing-Driven Approach

Here are some of the key elements of a marketing-driven approach:

Offer Something Without Strings

A marketing-driven approach is about focusing first on creating a connection. Ironically, in a sales-driven culture, direct marketing is often ineffective, but it can be highly effective when embedded in a marketing-driven business.

For instance, it is common in a sales-driven culture to develop a seminar without any input from C-level executives. This is counterintuitive to a marketing-driven culture because of its customer-centered emphasis. Besides, a poorly attended program is a waste of time and money.

In a marketing-driven organization, someone from your organization will want to talk to several executives in the process of creating an executive briefing. By doing this, they will probably get some excellent ideas for making the topic more compelling, and the executives may be willing to talk up the event to several other executives on the attendee list.

CONNECT WITH CUSTOMERS

The regional accounting firm of Barnes Dennig & Company, Ltd. was an early pioneer of providing educational events to capitalize on the desire of clients to learn something that has immediate value to them. An educational event is also a great way to learn things about your customers and prospects you will never learn any other way.

If you visit their website, you'll notice they have specialized products for each market they serve. You'll also notice that all the markets they serve are related and that their clients sell to each other (which creates another reason for participants to attend). They started with one market and gradually added other closely-related markets. This is the prototype all small businesses need to strive for in order to create a high value exchange with their customers.

CREATE EMOTIONAL COMMITMENT

Rather than selling, an event agenda is based on a fundamental, but powerful, concept. If you offer a customer or prospect something of value (with no strings attached), it will reduce his or her defenses and create an emotional commitment to your organization.

This is an essential point (and a key distinction between being sales-driven and marketing-driven). Instead of trying to establish a relationship based on selling something to a customer, offering up something of value (such as a seminar) creates a dynamic in which the other party is disarmed by your willingness to focus on what's important to them.

A second benefit is that educational events (and other customer-oriented experiences) are great vehicles for explaining products and services not easily reduced to sound bites. Because these types of programs typically address some sort of fundamental challenge in the customer's organization, it's also possible to create content the participants can use immediately.

In short, being able to create a variety of experiences involving customers is becoming the Holy Grail of marketing. This is because once you reduce the customer's defenses, the selling process is collaborative rather than a tug-of-war between the salesperson and the buyer.

THE LIMITS OF THE SELLING PROCESS

Hopefully, I've convinced you that a marketing-driven approach is superior to the classical sales-driven approach. If you're still not convinced, let's look at the selling process in a sales-driven business.

Rob is a partner in a small consulting firm. He can't figure out why clients seem pleased with his work, but frequently do not give him the green light for another project.

Rob is good at selling. His approach to selling is to ask insightful questions that uncover the customer's pain and then show how his product solves the problem. If he can get the client to open up, the key executive at the table is usually able to articulate why Rob's solution will solve their problem.

Unfortunately the client has decided on another consulting firm but needs to demonstrate due diligence. Rob, of course, does not realize this. Rob needs this project to make his bonus. He has designed a series of questions to bias the client toward his solution. Notice that both the buyer and the seller in this conversation have an agenda.

Because the client sees Rob as column fodder, she will not engage in an open conversation about her challenge. This puts Rob at a distinct disadvantage. The client is making it difficult for Rob to learn enough to suggest a compelling solution.

Later that day, Rob and his partner toss around the idea of hosting an executive briefing as a strategy for developing a deeper relationship with clients, but they are intimidated by the idea of speaking to a group of

C-level executives in the six markets they serve. They are concerned they may not be able to answer tough questions.

IMPLICATIONS

The sales-driven approach has gotten Rob and his partner to where they are, but it will not create the fly-wheel effect they need to grow. A sales-driven approach is simplistic. It starts with the mindset that being in six markets is better than being in one market. Here are just a few of the glaring problems that Rob and his partner face.

RESULTS OF ROB'S SALES-DRIVEN APPROACH

1. Every few months the well is dry.

2. No effort is made to build credibility as a thought leader.

3. The partners are vague about how their offerings fit together.

4. Nothing about their product offerings has changed in three years.

5. They have no idea what their customers really think of them.

Let's contrast this with a consultant who decided to focus on one market and create a marketing infrastructure.

By incorporating the five elements of a marketing infrastructure into his business, he automatically moved from a sales-driven approach to a marketing-driven approach. Best of all, he tripled his business in the last fifteen months.

1. Instead of pitching his business to a C-level executive over breakfast, he presents to C-level executives at conferences in his market.

2. His firm regularly conducts benchmark studies on hot topics in his market. This provides the content for his presentations and is a source of new business.

3. He is often quoted by Industry Influencers and he has authored several articles in journals aimed at C-level executives in his market.

4. He has used the information gleaned from customer dialogues to improve his products and services.

5. He recently partnered with the leading firm in the psychological testing field. This has resulted in several large referral contracts.

Chapter 5

End-Of-The-Chapter Questions

1. How do you create credibility?

2. Do you have a marketing infrastructure to your business? If not, what parts of it are missing?

3. If you don't have a marketing infrastructure in place, what questions will you have to answer before you can create one?

Part Two

Initiating Action (Chapters 6-15)

This section opens with a story about a "marketing challenged" organization that uncovers a profitable new niche using phone surveys.

As is the case with many businesses, the first instinct was to improve the strategy by improving the current product line. Fortunately, in the process of doing some detective work to find out what customers were thinking, three things happened simultaneously: a profitable niche was uncovered, a new product was developed, and the organization discovered what they could do better than anyone else.

From there, this section offers an in-depth guide for implementing the five elements of a marketing infrastructure. This includes practical ways to create superior lead systems, to develop a laser-like focus on your ideal niche, and to create new products that solve the limitations of current offerings in your market.

This section will also walk you through working with Industry Influencers and reporters. Of course, once an organization has developed a marketing infrastructure it is in a position to expand by adding other, related niches or taking on an additional salesperson.

Chapter 6

Mapping Out A Path Forward

Strategy is the first dimension of creating a marketing infrastructure. In his highly acclaimed book *Good to Great*, best-selling business author Jim Collins demystifies strategy. He says that great companies figure out what they could do better than anyone else and then determine a way to get there. [7]

This is not a process for the fainthearted. As Collins points out in his book, it took Kroger twenty years to realize its vision.

But What If You Don't Have Twenty Years?

How can a small business apply these insights? You can't put your small business on hold while you conduct an internal debate about what you could do better than anyone else (which, in organizations without good customer data, results in "pooled ignorance").

Small businesses need to fast-track. The answer is to parallel process. The least expensive way to do this is to conduct a series of phone surveys and then meet (once a week if possible) to review the data with the leadership. Conducting the meeting as a facilitated dialogue is the most effective way to proceed.

Customer surveys uncover either a new product concept that a customer is willing to fund or a set of customers in a niche market who need a more customized solution.

Niche customers share some common trait. They are in the same market or there is something unique about the nature of their business that presents a common challenge.

In the next chapter, I will show you the questions I use to identify either a customer willing to fund a new product concept or a niche market that is interested in a customized solution. One of the keys to uncovering the key challenge is to ask good follow-on questions (this requires someone with high business literacy).

How One Organization Did It

Here is an example of how I helped an organization find an underserved market niche:

The executive director of a professional association and her team were out of touch with the members and the market. Consequently, they were not in a position to make intelligent decisions about how to expand the business.

About 90 percent of their programs and services were not selling. The Executive Director and her team decided to engage me to do phone surveys of their largest customers and then share the data each week with the director and her team.

The information I gathered was intended to serve as a guide to improving the value proposition of their offerings. They had three challenges: An under-developed marketing infrastructure, products that were not selling and zero profits.

Backing Into A Strategy

Here is what we did to create an effective strategy:

Phase 1: Planning

1. Convened the key leaders to work on the problem.

2. Narrowed the challenge to a problem definition.

3. Defined what we were not going to work on (We are not going to work on tangential issues like the fact that the marketing department's program for turning prospects into members is not working).

Phase 2: Implementation

1. Conducted extensive phone surveys of C-level customers in Fortune 500 and Fortune 1000 companies.

2. Reviewed customer data (and its implications) each Wednesday morning with the leadership.

Phase 3: Key Findings

1. Most of the members were in the service sector, but all the action is in the manufacturing sector.

2. About 45 percent of individual members were promoted to new responsibilities within three years; many left the association.

3. The monthly newsletter was well received because it features a respected author, but the staff has no mechanism in place for developing and maintaining their expert knowledge.

Phase 4: Results

1. The phone surveys uncovered eight Fortune 500 companies that want the client to do a major project involving a multi-year contract.

2. All eight companies consist of service-sector businesses with a production component embedded in their operations.

SUMMARY OF ACCOMPLISHMENTS

1. Found a profitable niche.

2. Created a lead system by continuing to conduct member surveys.

3. Eliminated most of the public programs (which were unprofitable).

4. Changed focus from unpredictable sources of revenue (such as the direct marketing costs of soliciting $140 memberships) to multiple contracts (each worth $200 to $500 thousand).

5. Isolated twelve markets in the same niche (organizations with a production component such as hotels and urgent care facilities).

6. Used the monthly member newsletter as a mechanism for promoting the success stories generated from work with clients.

7. Developed a vision for helping customers in this niche with other processes such as product development.

THE LEARNING ORGANIZATION

By landing on large internal training projects rather than the public programs of the past, we created an opportunity for mutual learning. This provided a chance to develop additional competencies in other areas with systematic processes (such as new product development).

Is it the truly visionary strategy of a Kroger or a Walgreen? No. We saw a practical opportunity to serve an underserved niche. As a bonus, by working directly with customers, the association is getting paid to improve their product mix and develop more insight into what makes their organization tick.

The most critical keys to success were twofold: using dialogues with members as a lead system and finding a niche with an immature solution.

TIPS ON DESIGNING THE PROJECT

1. In structuring a weekly meeting, it's useful to identify the specific problem you want to work on. It's also a good idea to identify what you are not going to work on (if you don't do that extraneous issues will crop up just as the group is becoming productive).

2. Don't get caught up in a debate on whether improving the product is a good starting point. If you focus on uncovering a niche (based on customer feedback), it will lead to an improved product concept.

3. If you have a large database of customers, you may want to identify companies that represent the range of customers you serve in order to find the ideal niche.

4. If you have products that are not selling, consider eliminating them. De-cluttering opens up new opportunities.

5. Discovering what you are not good at is often the breakthrough that leads you to what you can do better than anyone else.

6. If you don't have a lot of customers, conduct a benchmark study by interviewing prospects who fit the profile of your ideal customer (as you know it now).

7. Define the problem accurately. Confront reality.

Continuing The Momentum

When the leader of an organization decides to reinvent the business, he or she must make decisions outside their comfort zone. Almost all new product creations require new attributes that stretch the organization's capacity to support them. In businesses that have not had a lot of recent success, operating outside of the status quo is a foreign concept.

A chronically under-performing organization is usually an insular organization. When this is the case, another key challenge will be to become less insolated from the customer. In order to develop a new product concept, for instance, the organization may need to collaborate closely with customers.

This turns out to be one of the most difficult dimensions of reversing the fortunes of an under-performing organization. The desire to remain aloof from customers is often a key reason for past failures.

How, Not What

When working with clients, I encourage them to turn *what* questions into *how* questions. As Theodore Levitt points out in his book *The Marketing Imagination*, strategy is more about *how* than *what*. Why the distinction? The word *what* is very specific. *What* describes something we need to identify. The word *how* suggests possibilities; it asks for the specifics related to executing the *what*.[8]

What involves questions like *what* are our customers' key pains? In contrast, a *how* question revolves around things like, *how* are unmet challenges in our customers' businesses impacting their performance and *how* are customers' customers impacting our customers' businesses?

Breakthrough Thinking

This kind of questioning process led Senco Products, Inc., a privately-held $300 million toolmaker, to ask, "How can we stand out in a crowded market?" Senco recognized other vendors could produce a product close to the quality of its own in the "big box" retail environment, which emphasizes low prices.

This led to the conclusion that Senco needed to focus on a strategy of creating innovative products. In order to do that, it needed to transform its thinking by learning how the best organizations in the world approach innovation. Senco also needed to transform its old-line manufacturing culture. To do this, best-selling book authors from industry and academia, such as Tom Kelley from IDEO and Robert Sutton from Stanford, were brought in to present their ideas.

RESULTS

Gradually, these speakers began to make their mark. The vice president of marketing hired a woman who was an expert in observing how customers use a product. They added things to their current products, such as a tape measure embedded in a stapling gun. They got production employees involved in the design of new products and they moved a significant part of their manufacturing process offshore. All of these moves were unthinkable in the old-line manufacturing culture of the past. In year three, they developed fifty-five new products.

As a result, when you walk into the Senco section at Home Depot, sales associates immediately show you one of Senco's exciting new products instead of using the Senco product line to sell a less expensive product (as they did in the past).

What's even more interesting is that the old-line manufacturing culture did not really go away. Innovation was superimposed on the culture, so there is a duality of both cultures operating inside the organization (which I believe is the only way it could work).

CHAPTER 6

END-OF-THE-CHAPTER QUESTIONS

1. What can your organization do better than anyone else?

2. What is your greatest challenge?

Chapter 7

Talking To Customers And Prospects

The second dimension of creating a marketing infrastructure is the development of dialogues with customers. Customer conversations are the linchpin of creating a marketing infrastructure. There are enormous opportunities to capitalize on these simple conversations.

Perhaps the Johari Window is the best way to show why getting customer feedback is so important.

Johari Window

	Known to Self	Not Known to Self
Known to Others	1. Open	2. Blind
Not Known to Others	3. Hidden	4. Unknown

The four quadrants that constitute the Johari Window developed from the work of Joseph Luft and Harry Ingham. The name Johari Window was derived from the first few letters in their first names.

Application

The window is an effective way to show the various types of knowledge you can gain from customer dialogues. The key thing to remember is that customer conversations will provide a deeper insight into what you can do better than anyone else, and as a result, you can dramatically improve your decision-making ability in every area of your business.

Although it was intended as a diagnostic tool to study human interactions, I find the Johari Window is even more valuable as a mechanism for providing a business with objective feedback. One challenge a business owner faces is evaluating his or her business situation objectively.

As a director at the Center for Management at Xavier University (which is now Xavier Consulting Group), I noticed that CEOs had difficulty separating the symptoms of a problem from the root cause of a problem. This surprised me until I realized that they were too close to a situation to be objective and they didn't see their own role in the problem.

Interpreting Johari Window

Each quadrant represents a window into an individual and his or her relationship to the outside world. Here is how it applies in a business setting.

Quadrant 1—Open

Quadrant 1 represents what both the organization and its customers know. For instance, I know that my chiropractor is one of the leaders in noninvasive spinal adjustment techniques in Ohio and so does he.

Quadrant 2—Blind (the one that keeps executives up at night)

Quadrant 2 represents what is known to customers but not known to the organization. I think it is irresponsible for chiropractors to sell supplements without a medical background, but many engage in this practice. If this judgment is common among patients of chiropractors who sell supplements, this fits Quadrant 2.

Quadrant 3—Hidden

Quadrant 3 represents what my chiropractor knows about the direction of his business but has not shared with patients. For instance, he may plan to move his business to another address in the next year.

Quadrant 4—Unknown

Quadrant 4 represents something which is not known by either my chiropractor or me, but becomes clear as a conversation leads to a new insight for both of us.

Connecting The Dots

Phone surveys are the best means for confirming what is known and uncovering new information. It's a lot like putting together the pieces of a puzzle.

As you continue to foster customer dialogues, you will create a more complete picture (although there will always be some missing puzzle pieces). The ultimate purposes of a continuous dialogue are twofold: to identify a market that will pay a premium for your unique competencies and to make better decisions. Once you uncover a niche, you can add other related niches.

More experiential vehicles, such as events, usually work better after you have developed a baseline profile. The unique aspect of using events is that they provide information about a customer's business you are unlikely to learn any other way (particularly the politics of the organization).

Besides, if an organization is out of touch with its customers, it's not possible to design a compelling event until the things that keep customers awake at night are known. It may also take some due diligence to discover who is the most appropriate executive to invite to an event.

Because a phone survey is usually the best place to start, we will begin with that. In a later chapter, we will explore in detail how to design more experiential forms of gathering information, such as the Internet.

Designing Effective Phone Questionnaires

A structured phone survey ensures each respondent is asked the same set of questions. This preserves the objective nature of the interview.

A structured questionnaire generally consists of no more than four to six questions. This allows the interviewee to expand on a question without the risk that the interviewer will lose track of the questions.

The format can be a phone call or a one-on-one meeting. As a rule of thumb, asking customers to fill out online surveys does not lead to new business opportunities in a business-to-business environment.

In designing the questionnaire, you must consider the following factors. They are:

1. What are your objectives?
2. Who is the decision maker for your service?
3. What role does the person interviewed have in the sales process?
4. What kind of challenges can your organization address?
5. What else do you want to know?
6. If they have a project, who will be the key decision maker in that sale?

What You Can Learn From Surveys

In doing a lost sales analysis phone survey for a Fortune 500 OEM, I found that four of their key competitors had unique value propositions that formed the core of their strategies. For instance, one competitor provided loans below bank rates, another embedded a chip in each piece of equipment. This enabled the company to make off-site repairs.

I also discovered that the client's sales team bid on projects without the mandatory install base required to be a viable candidate. In fact, my client did not have enough existing equipment installed to qualify for consideration in about 20 percent of the sales situations.

This indicated an obvious disconnect between the sales and marketing functions within the seller's organization and between the seller and the buyer. It may also go a long way to explain why less than 10 percent of proposals for large dollar amounts were accepted.

No matter what your purposes, surveys will always improve your understanding about how your customer perceives you and how you add (or fail to add) value. Here's a list of all the possible things you may want to learn more about:

Common Phone Surveys

1. Customer Satisfaction: This is best used as an opening gambit to initiate a discussion regarding a customer's key challenges. It's important to remember customer satisfaction does not guarantee customer loyalty (and it's not usually what customers want to talk about).

   This approach does kill two birds with one stone. It helps you do a better job of linking your services to a customer's key pain and it provides an opening for generating more business.

2. Customer's Buying Cycle: This is used to learn more about how a prospective customer will make a specific purchase decision.

It includes things like the budget, user requirements, identification of competing vendors, decision criteria, and roles members of the buying organization will play in making the purchase-decision. This can also be used in developing a list of C-level participants for an event.

As a ready reference, the book *Strategic Selling* provides an in-depth description of each type of buyer in a selling situation (this includes the Economic Buyer, the User Buyer, the Technical Buyer, and the Coach).

3. Lost Sales Analysis (also called Competitive Analysis): In addition to understanding the true reason a customer purchased from a competitor, this is also one of the fastest ways to learn a great deal about competitors.

    You want to know the specific sales reasons for selecting another supplier (it's rarely price). This enables you to also learn how the competition positioned its product.

4. Benchmark Studies: This examines some critical aspect of the customer's industry so the customer can compare his or her business to the industry as a whole. The goal is to go beyond understanding some key dimensions of your customer's business to actually getting your arms around a key trend that may impact the way business is done.

    When I'm doing a benchmark study, I offer to send an aggregate summary of the results to the respondent. To generate a higher response volume, you might also consider partnering with an association; the results could then be published in its journal.

5. New Product Development: A common method for developing a new product or service concept is to conduct a benchmark study that uncovers the challenges and pains of your market. If five to seven smart customers ask for the same thing, you have spotted a new product opportunity.

Generally, asking customers in a focus group setting if they would buy a new product or service is not a good idea. Most people either tell you what you want to hear or what they'd like to believe.

6. Customer's Customer: The purpose of this type of survey is to learn what is driving your customer's business. For instance, you might think that a traditional manufacturing business like Senco might be focused on quality improvement practices. In fact, most of the focus is placed on developing innovative new products. Why? A significant part of their business is in the "big box" retail environment, where commodity products yield low profits.

7. Market Research: This includes things like exploring new market segments, identifying locations for regional offices, developing client success stories, and exploring partnerships or acquisitions.

8. Precall Preparation: This involves things like contacting an organization's suppliers, customers, and employees in preparation for an initial meeting with an organization. In some cultures, contacting employees is unacceptable.

SAMPLE PHONE QUESTIONNAIRE

Here is a sample phone questionnaire directed to the participant of an executive roundtable.

PHONE SURVEY

1. Two weeks after participating in our executive roundtable, what is your general reaction?

2. Are there some concrete ways in which the things you learned will be beneficial to your organization?

3. If yes, zero in on one key issue and ask if it is the key challenge.

4A. If yes, ask him or her to elaborate.

4B. If no, probe until you find another fit between his or her concerns and your solutions. Once you find it, say...

5. We have helped other organizations in similar situations (elaborate; get reaction).

6. If they are interested in learning more, ask who will be involved in continuing the discussion. Then ask if they can set up a meeting with all the decision makers. If they recommend a letter to someone else, ask if you can use his or her name.

CHAPTER 8

CREATING SUPERIOR LEAD SYSTEMS

A superior lead system creates a consistent set of new business opportunities and it enables you to learn more about your customers. Some lead systems are also designed to uncover sources of customer-funded new product concepts.

Well-designed lead systems should be positive experiences for your customers (or prospective customers). To achieve this, it may be necessary to combine two or three lead systems for optimum results (Scenario 1 in this chapter is an example of this).

KEY DESIGN CONSIDERATIONS

In initial conversations, I am often asked to suggest some sort of lead system for promoting a new product. I always find this question to be a bit of a trap.

If you try to answer the question, you will get the response "We tried that" or "That won't work because …" It sounds like a relatively simple question that anyone with a marketing background should be able to answer. It's not.

When considering a mechanism for generating more business, it's critical to understand how you will reach the decision maker and how the lead system meshes with other initiatives the organization has undertaken. You also need to have a handle on the execution capabilities of the organization.

At the Center for Management at Xavier University, it was not possible to develop articles in trade journals or elsewhere until we developed experience working directly with customers.

Conducting customer satisfaction surveys with recent participants of our public executive development seminars was the fastest, least expensive way to leverage the credibility we earned with managers and executives. This enabled us to uncover opportunities to provide customized management development seminars on-site (a product we had limited experience delivering).

Here are some of the key questions to consider in setting up any lead system:

1. What is your ultimate goal in developing a lead system?

2. How effective is your current system for generating leads?

3. Do your products fit together or do you have products with little synergy?

4. What is your organization's primary strength and what lead system will complement that strength?

5. What is your budget?

What Works And What Doesn't Work

As a rule of thumb, direct marketing is not appropriate in a professional services environment. This rule can be violated, however, if you have already established credibility. For instance, a professional services firm was able to establish phone dialogues with CEOs due to the integrity of their world-class monthly newsletter. This led to a new source of profitable business.

The following examples show both the successes and the pitfalls inherent in designing a lead system.

Scenario 1

A leading laser surgery company has hired an Internet consultant to create an online game. The company needs to educate consumers with concerns about the potential risks of laser surgery. Early buyers for laser surgery require less education because they are predisposed to trying something new. Later buyers are more conservative.

Many of the prospective patients for this kind of elective surgery are women. The company understands it will need to supply a great deal of information because women generally do extensive research before making significant purchase decisions.

The information will be provided in the game itself. The game will make learning about laser surgery more fun. A coupon will also be offered. The company plans to promote the game in conjunction with radio advertising targeted at people who fit the profile of the ideal prospect. The game will also include questions that will collect a more in-depth profile on each candidate. After it is completed, a bank of telephone operators will contact each individual to offer details regarding the coupon and other prizes. The objective of the phone call is to make appointments for a consultation. This approach proves highly successful.

Scenario 2

A "big box" remodeling retailer will sell more if it can showcase its products and improve upon the consumer's do-it-yourself skills. The company creates Saturday morning seminars for this purpose. Unfortunately, it's difficult to get people to a class. Customers have lots of competing interests on Saturday (and many customers are too tired or too busy to attend an evening session). Seminar attendance is spotty.

Because more than one-third of all U.S. households shop online, the "big box" retailer eventually decides to create do-it-yourself video tips on its website. The videos are a hit with consumers.

Scenario 3

A professional association intends to contact member facility managers in an effort to get a referral to the C-level decision maker for on-site facility manager training programs. This is a bad design. Facility managers are not oriented to selling. Furthermore, the association does not know the key pains of its members, and consequently, the association has no idea what problem these programs will solve. It's also not clear if it's a win for members to refer the association to their boss.

What Does It All Mean?

Certain types of lead systems tend to work better in the consumer market, while others work better in a business-to-business environment. For instance, while online video tips work well in a consumer situation this approach to education is generally less desirable in a business-to-business environment. One reason is that in-house events provide an opportunity for participants to conduct business. However, this doesn't mean that other consumer strategies should be rejected. In fact, by adopting an idea from the consumer space you may create an approach that gets noticed.

The above scenarios also illustrate that each piece must fit together. For instance, imagine your business involves helping CFOs manage their costs in a retail environment. To generate more leads, you plan a series of profiles showcasing your success stories in a leading journal aimed at CFOs.

You know that individuals with specialized degrees (such as CIOs, lawyers, plant managers) are often difficult to engage. The nature of their job often requires them to react and they tend to be introverts. So before launching a series of articles you will need to identify the "personal win" for each CFO you plan to profile.

If you blindly assume such a win exists, here's the kind of nightmarish situation you might create: A national association spent months cajoling five high-tech executives to participate in a panel discussion. The audience for the program consists of about ninety Fortune 500, 1000, and 2000 companies representing potential customers and service providers. To sweeten the pot, a local newspaper agrees to feature an article on the event.

In a last-ditch attempt to get the holdouts to participate, the association threatens to invite several key competitors to participate. The executives finally agree. The point, of course, is that having a conversation that highlights mutual interests would have clarified wins and avoided the risky last resort.

Bringing Customers To The Business

There are a number of motivations for bringing customers to the business. Regardless of objectives, there are some important considerations in designing an event and selecting the audience.

Trial Runs

An organization is interested in promoting a consulting product to local Fortune 500 and Fortune 1000 companies. Skeptical it will sell in its current form, I arrange several executive briefings. These involve nine or ten successful small-business owners I know personally. During the Q and A session, the participants provide the CEO with some practical advice for improving the product.

The upshot is that the client gets some solid ideas for making the concept more appealing and they don't burn up leads. As a bonus, they have the opportunity to test the effectiveness of using executive briefings to introduce the product.

Elaine Schneider

FIGURING OUT WHO TO INVOLVE

Every business is unique. Here are some of the considerations involved in thinking about who to include in the discussion and where it might lead.

If you are prototyping a new product concept, large companies are more likely to fund it. The downside is that large companies are often given large discounts and they can make demands that tax the resources of a business. For instance, one small-business owner signed a contract with Wal-Mart without realizing the contract required him to drop ship his product at every Wal-Mart in the United States.

If you are looking for sources of new business, keep in mind that mid-size companies often represent the most profitable segment of your business. If that's your objective, you will need to look at both volume and profitability in whittling down the list of potential sources of profitable new business.

Once you've narrowed down the list, you will need to consider relationships. Each stage represents a deeper commitment to your organization. For instance, a prospect may be the source of new business, a customer may fund a new product concept, and an advocate may fund a new product concept, provide referrals and offer a testimonial.

PLANNING THE CONVERSATION

It is always best to involve those you know well. You know how they will react; therefore, you can determine if they will make a positive contribution to the dialogue. If you invite someone you don't know, there is always a risk that person will sabotage efforts to engage the group. If you must invite someone you don't know, the role that person plays in his or her own organization, and the culture of that organization, will suggest how he or she will react.

Because the mix of personalities will either facilitate or impede the conversation, you must also consider who will represent your organization. You need a facilitator who can frame the discussion. He or she also needs to be open to input from the group. Anyone else from your business also needs to be a positive contributor, although a focus-group format can involve many people in your organization who can observe without being observed.

Here is how you might put together a group you intend to invite to a briefing of a new product concept:

1. Identify your top twenty customers by volume or profitability. Select from list based on three or four criteria.

2. Consider adding someone who will foster "possibility thinking" (such as a board member).

3. Add suppliers, customers' customers, and Industry Influencers (if appropriate).

INITIAL SALES MEETING

If the group you engage results in some selling opportunities, here are some keys to a productive first meeting.

TIPS ON THE INITIAL SALES CALL

1. It is imperative that the final decision maker be involved in the initial meeting. Their take on the problem usually rules.

2. The first meeting is your organization's opportunity to ask questions that will illuminate the benefits of your solution.

3. It's unlikely the prospect will have a good understanding of how to solve the problem (unless they have met with a competitor).

4. At the conclusion, ask the key C-level decision maker how your solution solves the key challenge that has been identified. If he or she does not provide a cogent answer, more work is needed before doing a proposal.

5. It is essential to clarify the prospect's internal decision-making process.

6. Your organization will not succeed unless a coach emerges to help navigate the politics of the customer's decision-making process.

Chapter 8

End-Of-The-Chapter Questions

1. Briefly describe what you do to generate leads.

2. Are you satisfied with your current lead system? If not, did this chapter generate any new ideas for a lead system? If so, list the new ideas.

Chapter 9

Rethinking Your Market

The third dimension of creating a marketing infrastructure is to focus on one market or niche you can dominate.

If you are currently in six markets, without a marketing infrastructure in place, focusing on one market will yield better results than a shotgun approach to marketing.

Breaking Point

Here are some key reasons an organization without a marketing infrastructure reaches a crisis:

1. Superficial knowledge of markets they serve.

2. Lack of a viable lead system.

3. Ineffective sales approaches.

4. Competitors with better products.

Market Segments, Niches and Cells

Before we look more closely at a market segment strategy, you'll recall that a market segment is an industry—for example, the insurance industry. A niche is a specialized industry within a market segment, such as businesses that sell car insurance. A cell is more specialized—for instance, a business that offers minimum-coverage car insurance.

The Case For Specialization

Company A specializes in outsourcing marketing services to software companies. Because the software industry has its own language, the fact that the two partners of the firm have a combined experience of fifty years is very attractive. Their combined backgrounds include public relations, direct marketing, and managing a sales force.

In addition, they are instrumental in creating a local software association. This provides visibility, credibility, and a lead system. By speaking at monthly programs, they are developing a regional reputation as thought leaders in their industry.

Company B has experience in nonprofit, insurance and professional services. The owner has a huge network and regularly meets with anyone who might have a need for a marketing consultant. Because he casts such a wide net, he does not have a well-developed set of services. In contrast, Company A has a data sheet describing each service they offer.

Company A has a 60 percent sales close rate and can point to sizeable contracts for marketing projects with virtually every software company of any size in the region. In contrast, Company B has less than a 10 percent close rate.

You, Your Product And The Market

The relationship between your background, your product or products, and deciding which segment is best is not a one-size-fits-all strategy. It varies with circumstances. In the Company A example, the specialized knowledge the two partners possess in marketing and software suggests an obvious relationship between their backgrounds, industry knowledge, and the product offerings they will create.

In contrast, another set of experienced consultants in the executive coaching field do not have deep industry-specific knowledge. Because they have customers in many markets, they will have to think their way to the right niche.

> *In order to uncover a single profitable market they need to consider all five dimensions of the marketing infrastructure in light of their core strengths and their decision criteria.*

Here are some of the key things they know:

1. Their executive coaching material works well in environments with overwhelmed executives working in bureaucratic structures.

2. They excel at making presentations and selling.

Of the five markets they are in, only one fits their criteria. The market they select is growing, has an immature solution, and offers easy access to C-level executives. Because they already have several big accounts in this market, they believe they can leverage their experiences with these accounts by making presentations at executive conferences in the same market.

Notice that their strategy was relatively weak, but their execution was strong. As I explained earlier, execution trumps strategy.

Beyond Market Segments and Niches

Sometimes policies (or the nature of the business) require that a business look beyond a specific market or niche strategy. For instance, at the Center for Management at Xavier University, we had a policy of working with any organization that called. This precluded us from limiting ourselves to just a few markets.

Ways To Specialize

Here is a summary of the various methods for specializing. Notice that as you move down the list, the product itself takes on a more important role.

1. Find a market with an immature solution. An executive coaching firm specializes in working with hospital executives who are dealing with the inherent bureaucracy and the slow decision making of a hospital environment.

2. Find an underserved sector. A national association discovers they can help service-sector companies (with a production component enbedded in their operations) improve key quality dimensions related to safety, food quality, and customer service.

3. Provide a specialized product for a specific industry. Two executives with fifty years of combined experience in the software industry offer full-service marketing services to other software firms.

4. Provide a specialized set of services in one geography. The Greater Cincinnati Health Council pools the resources of hospitals in areas of common need such as public relations, data management, human resources, and education.

5. Offer the same core product to different markets. The Center for Management at Xavier University packages their management training programs into three distinct programs for small, medium, and large businesses.

6. Serve unrelated segments (clinics, car care). A local entrepreneur specializes in teaching phone skills to businesses that must depend on a technician to acquire customers.

Focus Improves Products

Earlier, I shared with you the story of the association that was having difficulty attracting new members and filling public programs. The up-front investment in acquiring new members and promoting their public seminars yielded poor returns.

By finding a sector not easily served, we created a desirable new product for an underserved market with a minimal outlay of cash. This proved far more profitable than the pursuit of individual memberships and unpredictable public seminars. One contact to a C-level executive might yield a multi-year contract worth $500 thousand or more per year.

It also enabled the association to leverage its world class newsletter by offering to include a success story that highlighted work with a client.

Now, a cruise line client could send an article from the association's monthly newsletter to their travel agent customers. The article, for example, might outline the steps the cruise line was taking to address two key concerns of travelers: safety and the spread of flu and other viruses on the ship. In effect, the association was helping them directly in their public relations effort as a bonus.

Before

13 public seminars
$60K in overhead

After

3 public seminars
$4K in overhead
Multi-year contracts @ $200K+
Consultants paid at project completion

Focus Leads To More Products

At the Center for Management at Xavier University, we achieved similar results. Instead of just offering a public seminar series, we customized our basic product at minimal up-front expense. Small businesses used our public seminars, mid-size companies hired us to do customized training, and large companies hired us to be their virtual corporate university. (Cincinnati has ten Fortune 500 companies and seventeen companies in the Fortune 1000 category). We later expanded the corporate university program to include an executive education program.

The public seminars also served as a lead-generation tool for developing additional business. Here is a simple summary of how we created more products:

BEFORE	**AFTER**
Public Seminars	Public Seminars (lead system for…) ↓ Customized Training Corporate University Executive Education

HOW TO GET STARTED

Almost everyone who makes a successful transition into a more focused strategy starts by looking at what they can do better than anyone else. This makes sense when you consider that you are looking for a market that stands to gain the most from the unique strengths your product or service brings to the table.

Customer surveys, success stories, and some soul searching seem to be critical in making this transition. There are usually some burning questions that need to be answered with new (or more) data before you can land on a solution. Often, someone in your organization is qualified to get this data.

Elaine Schneider

Why Staying On Top Is So Challenging

Here are just a few of the reasons small-business owners are challenged:

1. Customers expect more from products and services over time.

2. In the start-up phases of a business, the idea for the business often comes from previous work experience and customers. In later phases, the owner no longer hears firsthand what customers are thinking. New product ideas frequently come from conjecture rather than customer feedback.

3. Internal business processes quickly become sacred in both the customer's and the seller's organizations. As internal business processes become rigid, the organization becomes inflexible.

4. Social, political, and local events can have a significant impact on a business. If you don't stay informed, there is a risk that you will be operating on assumptions that are no longer valid.

Laurie Althaus, a certified business coach for Action International, agrees. She urges small-business owners to work on their business, not just in the business. If you are working on your business and not just in your business, you are also working on yourself.

This means reading, attending seminars, connecting with other small-business owners, and perhaps working with a coach.

Working on yourself improves your chances of eliminating attitudes that get in the way of your success and it improves the likelihood you will take effective actions.

Laurie cautions that working on yourself also requires a change in how you see yourself as the owner of the business. If you don't change that, the new attitudes and actions will not last; you will fall back into the same old habits (more about this in the last chapter).

Chapter 9

End-Of-The-Chapter Questions

If you are in a number of markets and wish to concentrate on one market or niche, these questions will help:

1. Which is stronger, your proprietary business knowledge (such as accounting) or your knowledge of a particular market?

2. Is the market that you understand the best growing?

3. What percentage of your customers are in this market?

4. Identify ten ideal customers in this market (based on factors such as revenue, location, etc.). This may require some research.

Chapter 10

Growing Beyond One Market

Once an organization has succeeded in creating a marketing infrastructure, it is in a position to expand the business by working with other related markets.

Vertical Markets

These related markets are called vertical markets. For instance, if you provide patient data to the hospital market, other vertical markets include the following:

1. Other businesses that mirror hospitals (an outpatient surgery facility).

2. Businesses that have similar operations (nursing homes).

3. Businesses that supply to the hospital (such as medical device companies).

4. Businesses that monitor hospitals.

5. Government sector.

OPTIONS FOR GROWING YOUR BUSINESS

There are actually a number of options for expanding the business at that point. They are: work with several vertical markets, pick a profitable niche within a market segment, expand into a new geography, or hire a salesperson.

WORK WITH SEVERAL VERTICAL MARKETS

The regional accounting firm of Barnes Dennig & Company, Ltd. works with industries that have a relationship to each other, such as manufactures, wholesalers, and distributors. It also works with businesses in the construction category. This vertical market includes architectural firms, general contractors, equipment suppliers, subcontractors, surveyors, and commercial realtors, to name a few.

Each new market the company entered was added only after a deep understanding of the current market had been gained. Much of the company's insight was developed by hosting a series of educational events; before anyone else in the industry was doing this.

They discovered it was a great forum for pooling new knowledge around common frustrations and that it provided ample opportunities for staff to acquire important new insights into customers' challenges.

Because their clients are architectural firms, general contractors, equipment suppliers, subcontractors, surveyors, and commercial realtors, they are also facilitating opportunities for clients to sell to each other (thus providing another incentive to attend their events).

PICK A PROFITABLE NICHE WITHIN A MARKET SEGMENT

LegalEase Solutions LLC provides high-quality, low-cost routine legal research. They are able to do this by outsourcing the work to India. They initially sold their services to small legal practices consisting of either a sole proprietor or several attorneys.

More recently, they have developed contracts with legal departments in large corporations by targeting corporations that require routine legal work (such as the fast food industry). This produces a more predictable stream of revenue.

Because all of the information is delivered via a secure Internet, they also have the opportunity to embed their services in the client's operation. This makes it far more difficult for the client to replace them.

Expand Into A New Geography

Not all businesses can remain local. For example, a marketing and consulting firm that specializes in the software industry can not survive in a midsize Midwest location without expanding outside the region.

The decision to expand the geography beyond the local level has two immediate implications for a small business: more expenses involved in acquiring additional customers and more difficulty in involving the customer in the business.

True, electronic communication tools are available, but offering an online discussion is a poor substitute for the kind of quarterly industry roundtables that Barnes Dennig & Company, Ltd. runs locally. A better solution might be to make presentations at key trade or professional associations.

In fact, finding out where C-level executives convene in your market (if they do) is an important consideration when evaluating a new niche.

Hire A Salesperson

If you decide to hire a salesperson (usually a commission situation) you need to provide the salesperson with the following things: success stories, scripts, a territory, leads (if possible), and product training. You will also need to walk them through your process for moving the sale to a conclusion (demo, pilot, etc.) and what happens after the sale. Most small businesses do not have the bandwidth to invest in sales training. If you do, you will want to provide a sales methodology and a sales process (as outlined in the books *Solution Selling* and *Strategic Selling*).

Of course, if you are expanding outside your current territory you will want to hire someone who resides in that territory so you can avoid housing costs and other expenses. If you can't provide leads, you may be able to provide a means of identifying leads. For instance, LegalEase Solutions suggests its sales representatives use LexisNexis (a free online research tool for identifying law firms by category and geography).

It is advisable to have a weekly phone discussion with your salesperson or sales team (if you hire more than one) to discuss progress. This is best done as a group over the phone, but it is hard to enforce mandatory attendance if people are paid on a commission basis. If they are able to pick up tips or you can provide leads, their incentive to attend will increase.

WHICH STRATEGY HAS THE MOST RISK?

Here are three ways a business can specialize. Which one has the most risk?

1. A specialized product for a specific industry, such as software.

2. Geographic specialization, such as a set of shared services for all the hospitals in the region.

3. A specialized set of products for small, medium, and large companies.

Number three has the most risk. This was the situation we faced at Xavier. Our mission involved servicing the entire business community. This meant we had to address the needs of a wide range of sectors, such as nonprofit, for profit, government, and manufacturing.

The solution we hit upon was to provide a distinct set of products customized to meet the unique needs of small, medium, and large businesses. The key to managing cost was being able to use the same baseline of materials. Only the format for delivery changed.

Why Number Three Has The Most Risk

The business community is always looking for evidence of expert knowledge. Because we were working with a diverse set of businesses, we had to leverage the experience of the faculty and outside consultants to improve the content and provide insight into the distinctions between sectors (such as manufacturing, nonprofit, etc.). At the same time, we needed a model that would ensure that our approach to management education was consistent. Here is a summary of the key things we needed to do:

1. Develop a working knowledge of the differences between the various sectors.

2. Stay current in specialties as diverse as management development, project management, and accounting.

3. Create a platform that enables the faculty and consultants to look for synergies between various approaches.

4. Develop a management model that provides a unified approach to management training and development.

Chapter 10

End-Of-The-Chapter Questions

As you contemplate generating revenue beyond your current capabilities, consider these three questions:

1. If you are in one market, is there enough business in your region to keep you busy?

2. If not, does it make sense to expand into the next region?

3. If not, are there related markets in your geography? For instance, a software company might grow by specializing in high tech. List them.

Chapter 11

Positioning Your Product

Positioning is a statement about who you are. It is based on three essential things: what you can do better than anyone else, your brand (or promise), and the market segment or segments you serve. Positioning yourself in the market clarifies who you are to anyone involved in the business.

From a communication perspective, positioning can be achieved with a twenty-second elevator pitch, success stories, and theme lines (such as "Good To The Last Drop"*)*.

How To Begin

There are a number of factors that can motivate an organization to reposition a business. It may be a lower close rate on new business, tired products, or a desire to increase profits (or all three).

Smaller organizations generally back into a repositioning strategy. They are looking for ways to get customers more excited about their offerings and ways to generate more profitable business.

The first step is to assemble all the relevant information available. It's like putting the pieces of a puzzle together. There is always at least one key concern that can only be addressed by talking to customers. If the organization is really disconnected from the customer, there will be many questions that must be answered before proceeding.

Sometimes the solution to a positioning problem involves finding a "middle way". As the earlier story about an association showed, being brutally honest about the growing indifference of service sector members (and the growing commitment of those in the manufacturing sector) created a new opportunity; working in service sector businesses with a production component.

Whatever the motivation for re-evaluating your position in the market, an effective repositioning strategy will involve all of the factors in creating a marketing infrastructure.

> As Phil Kotler says, "Great strategies consist of a unique configuration of many reinforcing activities…that are difficult to duplicate."[9]

Superior Products

The ideal way to position your organization is to create a superior product. Southwest Airlines broke the rules by going hub to hub in order to offer on-time business travel. Others, like Dell, improved on an inferior solution by offering the convenience of ordering a customized computer by telephone.

Before Dell created a way for customers to buy computers in the comfort of their homes, people had to get in their cars and go to retail stores that offered many types of computers. Once in the store, the customer depended on an overworked salesperson to help find the right computer.

Dell's solution improved the chance that customers would get a satisfactory solution. The chief reason for this is that phone conversations require a structured process for keeping the customer engaged. Furthermore, the organization can monitor the conversation to ensure the salesperson is following Dell's needs-assessment process.

In contrast, it's virtually impossible for a retail store to monitor whether or not salespeople are developing the best solutions for customers. In fact, the entire basis for determining how well the salespeople are doing can only be based on overall sales volume.

You'll notice that all of these companies improved on what were clearly suboptimal solutions and significantly improved the customer experience.

Continuous Renewal

As we've already discussed, the first step in developing a new product concept is to create a dialogue with customers (or prospects). Customers often come up with product concepts that improve on existing products, but if you have deep proprietary knowledge, a customer may look to you to co-create a product that solves a difficult challenge for which there is currently no solution. This may be the genesis of a new-to-the-world product.

In general, organizations that have a marketing infrastructure in place find it easier to create new products on a continuous basis. They are able to constantly reinvent themselves without a crisis. On the other hand, they may not make the leap forward that an organization in crisis may make (particularly with a new leader). Impending doom lends itself to thinking outside the box.

Product Categories

There are four main types of product categories. They are: new-to-the-world, first-generation, second-generation, and line-extensions.

New-To-The-World Products

New-to-the-world products solve a problem in a new way. The best example is the PC, but Southwest Airlines and Dell fall into this category also. Any product or service that dramatically improves on existing solutions falls into this category. Notice that a common thread in new-to-the-world products is that they often create a superior delivery system. Here are some of the ways that organizations create new-to-the-world products:

1. See the future before it is well understood. (Coffeehouses in Europe inspired Starbucks).

2. Create a new product category (PC).

3. Create a new solution in a current product category (FedEx).

4. Supply something in short supply (Quality TV programming, such as *Friends*).

5. Acquire another company that enhances your market position (FedEx Kinko's).

6. Combine two distinct areas of knowledge to create a new product category (technology and law are combined in Westlaw).

First-Generation Products

Any product has what Theodore Levitt, in his book *The Marketing Imagination,* calls "a bundle of value specifications"[10] that we commonly refer to as features and benefits. This includes such things as delivery, price, warranties, and training. It is wrapped around a problem or improvement issue that the product or service addresses.

In the business-to-business sector, a viable first-generation product or service produces a set of outcomes related to improvements in cost, quality, profitability, or revenue.

Each organization must create a unique bundle of value specifications that resonates with its customers. To do this effectively, an organization needs to put together an offering in which all the elements of the product are complimentary (we'll talk more about that later).

SECOND-GENERATION PRODUCTS

Instead of developing a new-to-the-world product, you may want to turn your first-generation product into a second-generation product. A second-generation product offers significant improvements over the initial product and a more direct link to cost savings or revenue generation.

The need to develop a second-generation product occurs as customers become more sophisticated and more competitors come into your market.

If it is becoming more difficult to sell or if your competitors are offering the same or a better value proposition, you must create a product that increases your value.

LINE EXTENSIONS

Line Extensions are similar to the concept of a second-generation product. For example, a corporation wants to sponsor thirty executives in a virtual corporate university program. But instead of just focusing on management development, the corporation wants the university to include MBA-level programs. When Xavier agrees to do this, they are creating a line extension.

If they later decided to develop an executive education program consisting of MBA-level coursework, they are creating a second-generation product.

THE PROBLEM WITH FIRST-GENERATION PRODUCTS

All products and services move from generic to specialized.

> Most first-generation product solutions are based on faulty assumptions that do not provide a satisfactory outcome.

For instance, many clients felt it was important to expose supervisors and managers to management development training. Later, the same organizations wanted us to show how our training program improved the personal effectiveness of a group of supervisors and managers.

In other words, they realized that simply exposing a group of managers to management development content did not guarantee that anything would change. Unfortunately, changing behaviors is difficult to do. Real changes require individuals to be motivated and disciplined (and they must have the innate skills required to form the new behavior).

Unlocking A Second-Generation Product

It is often difficult to unravel from the faulty fundamental assumptions that formed the basis of your first-generation product.

> *One way out of this dilemma is to redirect your focus to a niche that will value what you are uniquely qualified to solve. This will lead you to a second-generation product that does not have the limitations of the original, first-generation offering.*

For instance, a Fortune 1000 company believed that a group of doctors in its system could dramatically improve the way they ran their office by participating in a year-long program featuring MBA-level courses.

Because the executive education program they wanted us to create was based on acquiring new knowledge and not new behaviors (and it was aimed at highly motivated professionals with advanced degrees), it was more likely to achieve the desired outcomes.

Characteristics Of A Stellar Second-Generation Product

Offers A More Customized Solution

A niche solution often involves repackaging the original product into a customized solution.

> This improved product often does not require much up-front overhead (because you are able to capitalize on what you've already created).

Recall that the association in the earlier example was able to develop large training projects with Fortune 500 companies by tailoring the content of its public programs. This required minimal up-front effort to customize.

Provides Complimentary Product Attributes

The product itself must embody complimentary features and benefits in order to provide a compelling reason to purchase. Let me give you a simple example of this principle in action.

My windshield is cracked. I need it replaced. After calling a number of glass repair shops I am down to two possibilities. The first shop offers original manufacturer glass with a one year warranty. The other competitor manufacturers the glass (which is a negative) but backs it up with a lifetime warranty. It is also seventy dollars cheaper to install.

The second competitor has addressed a key concern: "How do I know your glass is safe if the glass is not made by the original car manufacturer?" By offering a lifetime warranty, they have solved a potential quality concern with a complimentary product benefit—a lifetime warranty. By making it cheaper, they have provided another incentive to purchase from them.

One simple way to confirm whether you have complimentary product attributes is to listen carefully to objections during the sales process. If you have a customer service function, it is important customer service representatives record questions or concerns voiced by customers and prospects. Salespeople, of course, can and should review calls they make to determine whether they are adequately addressing customer concerns.

Once you have listed all the objections provided from as many areas of the organization as possible, look at the organization's response. Is the answer adequate? If not, it is important to address the objections in order to develop more robust product features and benefits.

ADDRESSES PAST INADEQUACIES

A second-generation product takes into account all the factors that are present to create a whole product solution. This may include things like financing, consulting, training, maintenance, or outsourcing. It also addresses past weaknesses of the first-generation product.

Going back to the Xavier example, we knew that our management development training improved when participants returned for follow-up sessions, but this was not something clients were willing to support.

As we experimented with a virtual corporate university format, we realized that follow-up could be embedded in the process because participants attend a series of sessions over the period of a year.

In addition, it was far more practical. Clients readily agreed to permit participants to bring real problems to the sessions. This enabled the group to help each other improve the overall effectiveness of their organization.

IS MORE PROFITABLE

Because the buyer and seller are both aware of the inadequacies of a first-generation product, a second-generation product that passes muster with the buyer has a better impact on the bottom line. Furthermore, if the buyer is involved in shaping the final product, the buyer is willing to pay significantly more for the solution.

DOESN'T HAVE A HIGH-RISK PROFILE

Another reason to create products from existing products is that only about 10 percent of all new products succeed.

Robert Cooper, who is widely recognized as an expert in product development, conducted studies that showed most new ideas fail because not enough time and effort is spent making sure that the new product is something customers actually want. [11]

Most new product concepts are created in a vacuum by the leader. If a small-business owner is still heavily engaged in selling more business, new products are grounded in customer needs, but that is often not the case.

As the business grows, the demands of the business take over, and the business owner is getting anecdotal information about the customer. A disciplined approach to developing true insight into the customer's business is lacking. This shows up when business owners frequently admit they don't know the key pains of their customers.

Unless the small-business owner routinely engages the employees closest to the customer in dialogue, it is difficult to develop new products.

First-and Second-Generation Can Coexist

A first-generation product can continue to be a viable product. Although public training programs in supervision and management at Xavier lack the breadth and depth of other programs, they continue to be viable due to the fact that organizations want to provide new supervisors and managers with an overview of their new responsibilities, and they need a convenient way to do it.

At Xavier, the public seminar series is both a source of ongoing revenue and a lead system for other second-generation products.

Cannibalizing Products

I know of only one instance where a firm cannibalized its product. It occurred when the firm created a second yearly conference. Because they were not intimately familiar with the challenges of their customers, they created a conference that had a different title but covered the same ground as their other conference.

Cannibalizing products will rarely happen to you if you think in terms of new delivery systems and whole-product solutions. In the professional association market this might include public seminars, customized training programs, web-based programs, and conferences.

COMMON ELEMENTS OF SECOND-GENERATION PRODUCTS

Here is a list of some of the ways to create a second-generation product:

1. Customize a product for a specific market or niche.

2. Develop a new way to deliver a product.

3. Create a product that allows a customer to outsource a process that is not a core competency.

4. Embed technology in a product to improve its value proposition.

5. Add a service to a product or a product to a service.

Chapter 11

End-Of-The-Chapter Questions

What categories do your products fit into?

Category	Product Name
New-to-the-world	
First-generation	
Second-generation	
Line extensions	

Chapter 12

Developing New Products

Products and services are constantly evolving. In the early days of mystery shopping, for instance, employees were evaluated on how well they performed in a customer interaction. Today there are thousands of programs. In the business-to-business sector, a typical mystery shopping service might include monitoring phone calls with customers, coaching, training, testing, and hiring.

If you are creating a new product without the benefit of a customer who is willing to fund the new product concept, here are some practical ways for small companies to develop a product with limited resources.

Fast-Track Product Development

The key is to parallel process: To parallel process, you must do four things at the same time: market tests, technical assessments, financial analysis, and early prototypes.

Once you have a crude drawing, model or methodology, you will want to test it (prototype it) with customers. Here is a snapshot of the product development process.

Market Testing

1. What evidence suggests this is a product customers want?

2. What key pain will this product solve for the customer?

3. Is the product a source of competitive advantage?

4. Does it meet the unique needs of our market segment or niche?

5. Is it profitable? How profitable? What kind of income will it generate?

6. What does a market analysis show (market size, growth, trends, competition, segmentation)?

Technical Assessment

1. Is it feasible?

2. Can it be developed with existing R&D capabilities?

3. Are there patent issues?

4. What is the timeline for product development?

5. What are the agreed upon outcomes at each stage of the product development process?

Financial Analysis

1. Costs of development?

2. Projected revenue and demand?

Early Prototype (drawing, proposal, methodology)

1. Test concept with customers (face-to-face interview with prototype, including product descriptions, crude models, and pricing).

2. Determine if the product or service works within the customer's business. Can it be embedded?

3. Adjust as needed.

Co-Creating Products

As customers become more sophisticated about what a second-generation product might be able to do, they often partner with suppliers that have competencies that set them apart from the competition.

> *Their objective is to co-create a product that will either enable them to gain a strategic advantage over their competition or solve a persistent problem that is making them less competitive.*

For the supplier, this represents the opportunity for either a new-to-the-world or second-generation product that offers a superior set of interlocking features and benefits.

The customer will often attempt to limit your ability to commercialize your product to a wider audience, particularly if they see this product as the source of competitive advantage. The customer is, of course, functioning as a visionary buyer.

If you can create a product with unique capabilities, your organization will have gained new competencies that competitors will find difficult to duplicate.

Why Some Suppliers Are Reluctant

Not all suppliers are comfortable with the concept of co-creating a product. Here are some of the reasons:

1. Suppliers are used to creating products with little thought given to how it fits into the customers' organization.

2. Like customers, suppliers don't like changing their internal business processes.

3. Developing a new product concept requires an organization to move out of its comfort zone.

4. Suppliers fear showing their ignorance in front of customers.

ADDITIONAL DUE DILIGENCE

Additional considerations in co-creating:

1. Does the customer agree you can sell the final product to other customers?

2. Who will sponsor this internally in both organizations? Who will be involved in the design?

3. Is the customer paying the development costs?

4. Could this product form the basis of other products?

SIMPLE DECISION CRITERIA

If the customer is funding the project (and the above four questions are addressed to your satisfaction), you may choose to streamline the decision process if these five things are true:

1. It's a service.

2. It can be created quickly without major modifications.

3. It addresses a key pain of other customers.

4. It is highly profitable.

5. The customer is reasonable.

Customer's Criteria For Product Acceptance

There are a several factors that predict whether or not a new product will be accepted in the business-to-business sector. Some key considerations from the customer's perspective are:

1. How well does it address our challenge?

2. Is it a whole product solution?

3. Does it fit within existing processes?

4. What are the up-front investment requirements?

5. When will this product pay for itself?

6. Who will champion the implementation of the new product in the organization?

7. Does the supplier have credibility?

8. What do Industry Influencers think?

9. What kind of experience will we have with this supplier and this product?

Putting On Your Game Face

When working with a beta-site customer, your weaknesses are bound to show up. Here are some of the glaring negatives that I have seen small-business owners engage in:

1. Acting without any sensitivity to other people's time.

2. Not treating members of the customer's organization with respect.

3. Not keeping customers informed.

4. Reneging on agreed-upon product changes.

5. Not being open to ways to improve on the product.

Everyone knows that customers avoid suppliers who disrupt or upset their employees. If an organization is perceived as being difficult, people talk. Other companies in the same market will think twice about using that organization. Yet, some small-business owners make the mistake of thinking that the C-level executive who approved the project is the only one who counts.

The manager who is actually using the product (the User Buyer) is in the best position to create new business opportunities. He or she is also able to provide an objective perspective on how the product meshes with internal business processes and suggest ways to embed the product in the operation. This, of course, makes it more difficult to eliminate the product. This is the good news.

The bad news is that if the User Buyer does not like a supplier, he or she will find a way to sabotage further business opportunities and will share his or her point of view with colleagues.

If a small business is operating in one or several niches, this reality must be part of the equation in managing customer expectations.

In business, you never know who can help you. The person you think is in the best position to help often can't (or won't), but someone who may not seem important can be the key to unlocking a new opportunity.

Chapter 12

End-Of-The-Chapter Questions

1. What was the last new product you created?

2. How did you get the idea for the product?

3. How did you test its feasibility with customers?

4. What about prototyping a new product concept by creating a drawing or model? What are some other ways that you could make a new concept more tangible to the customer?

Chapter 13

Industry Influencers and Public Relations

This section will provide an overview of the fourth dimension of creating a marketing infrastructure—working with Industry Influencers.

An Industry Influencer is anyone whose opinion carries weight in an industry or discipline. This includes (but is not limited to) writers, editors, publishers, reporters, and trade groups. They are the experts who write, speak, and make connections that impact how people view your product.

Public Relations (PR) involves publicity, promotion, opinion making and public affairs. PR employs a subtle approach to educating customers and prospects on the benefits of your offerings. Public relations includes things like newsletters, conferences, articles in trade magazines, and sponsorships.

Working with lawmakers at a state, local, or federal level is also a critical element of the mix if you are a nonprofit group; if you are in a heavily regulated industry; or if you are selling to the government. However, we will confine our focus to the publicity, promotion and the opinion-making aspects of public relations and leave the lobby activities to firms that specialize in that area.

This chapter will help you evaluate your current approach to working with Industry Influencers, and it will assist you in evaluating any individuals or consultants involved in your public relations efforts.

If you plan to manage public relations yourself, this section will provide you with a road map. No matter how you proceed, it's absolutely essential to make sure every aspect of your PR effort supports the sales process.

Public Relations Is Relative

Everything you do in public relations depends on your objectives, the nature of your business, and your core marketing strengths. If you're a professional services firm, for instance, building credibility through public relations is usually more effective than direct marketing.

Getting quoted in the *Wall Street Journal* may be easy if your business involves rating hospitals, but it may be more difficult if you specialize in coaching hospital executives.

On the other hand, something as mundane as a facilities management business can be turned into material on how a firm is dealing with threats like terrorism.

How Public Relations Works

A small business may use local publicity to promote its business and trade journals and national newspapers for opinion-making purposes. Local publicity takes the form of sponsorships, proprietary events, and local media coverage. Opinion making is more substantive and usually involves national or international exposure. It includes things like:

1. Presentations to C-level executives at a national association meeting.

2. Press conferences at trade shows for things like announcing a new product.

3. Trade journal articles regarding successful work with a customer or new trends.

4. Quotes by you from reporters who regularly write about your industry in places like the *Wall Street Journal* or the *New York Times*.

5. An in-depth report on results of a benchmark study.

If you would like a well-placed article in *USA Today*, the key is to identify the reporter who covers topics related to what you do. If the publication does not provide that information, notice who writes those kinds of articles.

If you are planning an article in a trade journal, you must talk to the editor. Your main objective is to get the editor's blessing on an angle for the article.

To prepare for the conversation, it is important to study back issues and to get a copy of the publication's editorial calendar. This will tell you what trends will be covered and how the publication looks at issues. When working with the media, it is also critical to understand their deadlines and time pressures.

THE FOUR CONSIDERATIONS

Before landing on a pubic relations strategy, there are four key elements to consider. They are: industry expectations, relationships with Industry Influencers, complexity of product, and your internal branding process.

As stressed before, some organizations are better positioned to capitalize on the multiplier effect of endorsements.

INDUSTRY EXPECTATIONS

In some industries such as software, public relations is the expected communication protocol. This takes the form of a media kit consisting of success stories from customers, news on new product introductions, and endorsements from Industry Influencers.

The importance of PR can't be overemphasized in other areas, such as consulting. Other forms of promotion, such as direct marketing and advertising, are usually less effective (unless they are done in conjunction with public relations). This is due to the fact that leading with a direct marketing approach violates the accepted protocol of the industry.

Relationships With Industry Influencers

Who functions as the Industry Influencers in your market? This includes thought leaders, executive directors of associations, and reporters for the Associated Press and other media outlets.

Industry Influencers are useful in gaining access to customers directly through their publications. Association executives may also provide an introduction to prospective customers.

A marketing firm specializing in the software industry may not find the American Marketing Association useful as a lead system (because only a small fraction of their members represent software companies). They may, however, find that affiliating with a software industry trade association leads to new business opportunities.

Complexity Of Product

Complex products provide an opportunity to educate customers. Simple products don't. Educating customers can also lead to publicity. For instance, a regional accounting firm may host a quarterly roundtable for executives in the construction industry followed up by a summary in an industry-specific publication or a local business paper.

Internal Branding Process

There are two dimensions to internal branding: The first element is speaking with one voice. This is accomplished by displaying and talking about your twenty-second elevator pitch, value proposition, and success stories. The second dimension is providing ongoing education for employees, suppliers, and customers. This is especially critical if you have a complex product.

Ineffective PR

Scenario 1

A local liberal arts university specializes in providing university degrees to adults who have some college experience (similar in concept to the University of Phoenix). Students can usually matriculate within two years if they work on a full-time basis.

The student body is diverse, but predominately female. Only about 20 percent of the students are male. About 70 percent are African-American. There are a number of large companies that sponsor students.

The public relations office is in charge of marketing the university. Because many people in the region are not familiar with the university, the PR department initiates a series of articles on the university in a popular local newspaper.

Unfortunately, the university has a name similar to that of another local institution. This leads to some obvious confusion that readers are unlikely to sort out over morning coffee.

The pubic relations department also spends a great deal of money on a new logo and new business cards, but neglects to do anything about the barely visible sign for the main campus driveway.

Because the public relations office has done nothing to link promoting the university to bringing in more students, the burden of selling the program to potential students falls to others who have no expertise in marketing and a scant budget.

In an effort to rectify the situation, an already overburdened dean hosts a two-hour overview of the program on campus (and at some sponsoring organizations), but the university doesn't have the resources to diligently follow up with participants.

> *This is frequently the situation in organizations without a marketing compass. They spend lavishly on ineffective promotional strategies, and then—when they finally come up with a realistic plan for generating leads—they no longer have the resources to do it right.*

The key problem (in a nutshell) was that the public relations strategy was not linked to the selling process or a marketing infrastructure. The lack of a marketing infrastructure shows up in things like the lack of a student profile and the ineffective use of Influencers. They also lack nitty-gritty tactics that would generate some concrete leads.

Because a significant number of the students are members of several large churches in the area, the university might host a gathering to honor the current students and alumni after Sunday services.

Similarly, when a new student signs up, the university needs to find out who approved it in the sponsoring organization. By working with that individual, they can arrange a short presentation to a larger group of employees at lunch.

There are three important observations about this plan. They are:

1. Influencers (in this case) consist of local ministers and sponsoring companies.

2. The lack of a robust student profile hampers current promotional activities (because they know virtually nothing about their customers).

3. They need to open an office on the campus of the local community college since it awards most of the associate degrees in the region.

Scenario 2

The chief marketing officer of a professional services firm was profiled in a local business journal for working with her staff to consolidate all of the local charities they sponsor. This is a good way to begin rationalizing the PR process, but it does not go far enough. The CMO is looking at what causes the staff is most passionate about, but it is not that simple. All PR activities must pass the acid test of determining if the activity will bring in more business.

Sponsorships create noise, but noise will not translate into more business unless it is linked in some way, shape, or form to your identity. If a promotional activity is unrelated to your identity, you also risk that your message will become associated with another firm. Frequently, when consumers are asked to recall a message they remember the content of the ad, but they credit it to a competitor. Beer commercials are a good example of that.

A small-business owner can defocus the business in the same way. For instance, the CEO of a small software company committed his organization to ten days of building homes for Habitat for Humanity. Another CEO got involved with chamber activities designed to improve the business climate in his region. Neither effort had any relationship to the bottom line. Both organizations went out of business a year later.

Procter & Gamble has the bandwidth to engage in community activities that make the region more attractive to recruits. Small companies don't have the luxury of this type of long-term investment strategy. When a small-business owner does more than the organization has the bandwidth to do, it erodes the logic of the business.

Effective PR

Here are two examples of public relations at work. The first example shows the value of public relations in creating credibility and gaining visibility. The second example shows the role of public relations in publicizing a new product.

Scenario 1

A local shoe store called The Running Spot specializes in running shoes. Every year, this small business is a sponsor of the Flying Pig Marathon in Cincinnati and smaller local running events, such as the Heart Mini-Marathon.

Scenario 2

A local chamber wanted to create a new vehicle for providing educational programs for its mid-level members. It developed a speaker series featuring best-selling business authors. To generate interest within the business community, it did three things:

1. Worked with a local bookstore to find a publisher willing to sponsor best-selling business authors on a quarterly basis.

2. Invited three large associations to participate. In exchange for lists of members, each association was encouraged to have a promotional booth.

3. Worked with local reporters to get an article regarding the series in local publications weeks before the event.

This resulted in a profit of over $10 thousand for each event and netted a database of over one thousand qualified potential members.

Not All PR Is Good

A local newspaper has published a series of articles on the million-dollar bonuses of the key executives of a retail clothing merchandiser. Their sales associates must wonder why they are paid so little. Shoppers must wonder how much more they are paying to support these bonuses.

Elaine Schneider

Handling Negative Publicity

The most important aspect of pubic relations is to avoid a superficial response. It leads to more cynicism. Rather than spinning a story, everyone involved in managing the response needs to address the underlying cause of the controversy by taking concrete steps to address the problem.

In responding to questions from reporters, talking points are useful. These help to reframe questions so you can make the points you want to make (regardless of the actual question). Observing how politicians answer questions is useful in learning how to develop both skills.

It's also important not to engage in a war of personalities in the press. Patricia Dunn, former chairwoman of Hewlett-Packard, made a strategic error in not remaining above the fray when HP's techniques for investigating leaks by board members came under scrutiny.

Before You Hire A Publicist

Goals

Before undertaking any PR, it is critical to develop clear goals. Goal setting needs to be worked out with the board's involvement.

Role Of The Publicist

It is important that the board, executives, and staff know that the publicist is the only person who should approach the media. This means that the publicist must know what is happening in the organization. Nothing can impact the credibility of your organization faster than leaving the publicist flat-footed when the media calls.

Internal Communications

The publicist needs to work with the leadership to develop a consistent message. This is always a work in progress (because all businesses change). It is critical to make sure everyone associated with the effort is clear on the basics, such as the positioning strategy, the twenty-second elevator pitch, and success stories.

KEY INFLUENCERS

In the hospital and software industries, there are specific watchdog industries that evaluate the industry as a whole. For instance, most hospitals submit information in hopes of being identified as the best in one or more categories by organizations that rate hospitals.

Because many hospitals meet the *best* standard in at least one category, this type of PR can't be ignored. In addition to providing credibility, it serves as the source of positioning in the region. Each hospital specializes in certain areas in order to capture most of the business in a specific specialty.

EXPOSURE TO C-LEVEL EXECUTIVES

What is the best way to gain exposure to C-level executives in your industry? The answer to that question depends on where you find final decision-makers. For instance, for LegalEase Solutions, final decision-makers are found at the American Bar Association's annual trade show.

Unfortunately, in some industries, C-level executives do not conveniently convene at certain events. To address this issue, some industries create their own proprietary events. The statistics show that industries like health care, financial services, and software are spending less on traditional promotional strategies and more on hosting events.

CONTENT

If you're planning an article in the business section of a local morning newspaper, be aware that people will be reading this over morning coffee. You must also match the content to the reporter and the newspaper. Local business reports are not comfortable with business content that could leave some readers confused. It's also helpful to

Elaine Schneider

know the format the reporter will be using (such as an interview Q and A format).

Carving Out A Thought Leader Role

The CEO of a division of Hershey spoke out on the need for the coffee industry to regulate itself. He argued that if they didn't, the government would. His comments were included in a newsletter to all business-to-business customers (this division provided coffee and other vending food products to business).

His role as a thought leader created the perception that he is the leader in quality coffee products. This approach was even more effective than customer testimonials or other more self-serving forms of advertising.

For Better Results, Embed Direct Marketing in PR

You'll recall that in an early section of the book, I talked about the growing disenchantment with direct marketing and advertising. Though both (as stand-alone promotional tactics) produce inferior results for many organizations, traditional promotional strategies need to be embedded in the PR process in order to link the PR back to the sales process.

For instance, if you intend to generate new business from an event, the person managing your PR will need to promote the event and then contact participants after the event. Without follow-up, there will not be a next step.

Here are some examples of the use of direct marketing as part of a public relations effort:

1. Phoning executives during the planning stages of a conference to test the level of interest in the topics and get their commitment.

2. Phoning editors to discuss an article (it never works to write a general article on a topic and hope that a trade journal will pick it up).

3. Inviting Industry Influencers to a product introduction at an industry trade show.

4. Using telemarketers to identify the decision maker prior to hosting a C-level educational event.

STRATEGIES FOR CONTINUOUS PUBLICITY

One strategy for creating ongoing publicity is to institute something that occurs on a regular basis. Karen Sams, public relations manager at Misukanis & Odden, did a series of articles spaced over a six-month period for a leading project management journal. Her angle was to do a monthly article featuring one of the six critical success factors of being an effective project manager.

The Center for Economic Education, housed on the campus of the University of Cincinnati, develops a yearly report on economic conditions in the region. An association that caters to C-level executives publishes the results of an ongoing series of surveys to CEOs.

But what if you can't find a reporter who handles your industry? A regional law firm hosts a quarterly panel to discuss trends that affect general counsels. Unable to find a reporter who covers this area, they create a four-color insert that summarizes the results of the event. It falls under the category of advertising, but is written just as a reporter might describe it in the local business paper. It has the added advantage of being eye catching.

Chapter 13

End-Of-The-Chapter Questions

1. Who are the key Industry Influencers in your market?

2. List some realistic ways you might improve your relationship with these Influencers.

3. List your key strengths in marketing. How can these strengths support cultivating a relationship with Industry Influencers?

4. If public relations doesn't fit within your marketing competencies, do you have the resources to outsource it to a PR firm?

5. If so, are there ways you might support the PR effort? For instance, if you are strong in direct marketing, you will want to make follow-up contacts to participants after an event.

Chapter 14

Working With Reporters

If you are a small business, you may not have the resources to hire a public relations firm or a publicist. Or you may feel that you are the best person to direct PR. For this reason, I have included a lot of detail on working with reporters and getting the most from the effort.

The Basics

I've noticed people from a sales background are usually very good at PR. Salespeople intuitively understand public relations must be practical. Here are three concepts they understand very well:

1. PR is used to generate more business.

2. Publicity requires you to cold-call reporters and Industry Influencers.

3. Communications must be succinct and provocative.

Initiating Contact

A good way to gain access to a reporter is to find out if the reporter is doing a presentation or covering an upcoming event. If that's not fruitful, you can develop an e-mail correspondence with the reporter by commenting on a recent article (of course, the feedback needs to be positive). Some marketing directors routinely send out press releases. Press releases are never appropriate.

ANGLES

Angles are the most challenging aspect of publicity. To understand angles, we must first understand that there are three types of coverage. They are:

1. Hard – such as an article about an upcoming event.

2. Feature – such as a link between your product and a business trend.

3. Human Interest – such as a customer success story.

In addition, you must suggest several angles that are consistent with the types of themes the reporter covers and the preferred format (such as an interview format).

As an example, Joe runs public relations for an organization that provides data on the management of various diseases. The reports are developed for health care providers. He notices that there are a number of articles in the leading newspapers showing that deaths decreased in the past twelve months. He decides to develop an article explaining why there are fewer deaths. This angle will allow him to showcase the value of the data his business provides to health care providers.

KEEP IT SIMPLE

If a reporter asks for an e-mail outlining the various angles for an article, the entire correspondence should fit in one paragraph. Reporters are constantly reacting to what is occurring around them; they do not have time to read anything longer.

TIMING

If the article is time sensitive, the time at which the article will appear needs to be negotiated in the initial conversation. (Reporters tend to write the article a few days before the article will actually appear).

CONTEXT

It's important to frame the conversation to make sure that the reporter does not have an axe to grind and to explore the reporter's openness to the way in which you wish to frame the article.

COMMITMENT

Once the reporter agrees to do an article, your organization is locked in. The reporter is the ultimate customer. I never agree to do public relations for an organization before they agree to this ground rule.

Most reporters work on very tight deadlines. When things go wrong on your side, it often occurs at the last minute. This is a problem since the reporter has already planned and cleared the placement of your article. If you don't come through on your end, you will fundamentally change the dynamics of the relationship between yourself, your organization and the reporter. This could open the door to some negative publicity later.

This is also one of the reasons all calls regarding PR need to be referred to the individual handling public relations. This avoids miscommunication. If a speaker wants to renege on an interview, for instance, you don't want someone from the organization telling him or her that's not a problem.

DUE DILIGENCE

One way to virtually ensure that your business will get PR whenever you want it is to provide all the information a reporter will need to write the article. Reporters love to write, not dig for mundane details. To do this in a concise fashion, the PR person needs to understand the reporter's preferred format.

Once the reporter agrees to do an interview to promote an event, for example, the reporter will need an overview of the event topic, logistical details regarding the event, information on the interviewee, background on your organization, and a picture of the interviewee. If you have it, you may also want to include other interviews the subject has done. However, it is generally not a good idea to suggest to a reporter that they might want to use the same angle.

Internal Communication

One client regularly brought in best-selling authors to speak. Prior to the meetings, several people led prepared presentations of their books. Because the press, customers, suppliers, and prospective customers were invited to attend the events, we reviewed the organization's twenty-second elevator pitch and several talking points beforehand.

Execution

A publicist must always be thinking about what can go wrong. For instance, a reporter doing an hour-long interview on an NPR affiliate provided the audience with the incorrect phone number for our organization. Fortunately, the station patched me through seconds before the show ended so that I could give listeners the correct number.

Measurement

It is difficult to accurately measure the effectiveness of PR. Some argue that the minute you try to measure it, you've lost the battle. However, if your publicist is promoting an event, those answering the phone can find out how callers learned about the event and track caller comments. This makes the job of taking reservations more imporant and those doing it usually respond by providing helpful comments.

If you have an article in a trade journal, attaching a business reply card (BRC) will encourage readers to request more information. This doesn't capture all those who are interested, but you can follow the trail to the number of appointments and closes generated by this type of publicity.

There are other types of measurements available. For instance, publicists use surveys to track if there is an uptake in general awareness before and after a publicity campaign. However, awareness does not necessarily impact purchase behavior. General awareness campaigns should be avoided in preference to more direct methods of generating more business.

Preparing The Interviewee

Let's imagine an Industry Influencer will be speaking at an upcoming event you are hosting. You have arranged for a reporter to interview the speaker.

Because even seasoned speakers are concerned that they may look foolish in an interview, you need to prepare the interviewee. In initial conversations regarding an event, it is important to understand what your mutual interests are. This is because the speaker will try to renege on doing an interview about 20 percent of the time. By clarifying mutual interests, including the speaker's motivations, it is less likely he or she will try to cancel the commitment.

It's important to provide the interviewee with some insight into the reporter who will be interviewing them. Some newspapers have a policy of handling everyone with kid gloves (which is always a welcome piece of news) or the reporter may have some pet questions, like "Name your favorite books?"

If you can, provide the interviewee with other interviews or articles the reporter has done. The reporter will not have time to forward his questions beforehand.

Why Internal Branding Is So Important

Senior executives often resist the exercise of developing a consistent message.

> *Without a consistent message, every person in your organization is going to explain the company from the vantage point of what he or she does.*

This leaves anyone who is in contact with your organization with the distinct impression that your company does not have its act together.

Even more important, every opportunity to describe your business is an opportunity to sell. Consequently, you want to ensure that everyone is able to articulate the organization's key marketing messages. This includes a review of the mission of the organization (if you have one), the twenty-second elevator pitch, and several success stories. At Gus Perdikakis Associates Inc., every employee shakes your hand when introduced and immediately provides you with a business card. It is a very effective way of signaling their desire to do business.

SIMPLE WAYS TO IMPROVE COMMUNICATION

A good publicist will use the excuse of an upcoming event to assemble anyone involved. I find employees are very receptive to a pre-event briefing, especially if you provide free food. This is also a great way to kick off a weekly lunch featuring presentations from various members of the organization. It's particularly effective for teams to share what they are doing.

If you expect an immediate response to a publicity article, you need to have people available to take early-morning calls. If that is not feasible (for instance, if you are doing a Saturday interview), it's a nice touch to customize your voice mail to include some mention of the interview (and when calls will be returned).

It is important to make sure that everyone is armed with all the information needed to answer questions and to fill out information on callers. To make it concrete, a laminated "cheat sheet" containing all the relevant information on the organization (and responses to likely questions) can be used by the staff in responding to phone inquiries.

The staff needs to have a hand in creating the question-and-answer section. They have the most knowledge of the kinds of questions they get (and questions they have difficulty answering). If the staff is not involved in creating the laminated "cheat sheet," they will disregard it.

The owners of Twin Horizons Travel go one step further. They provide their staff with a copy of their weekly column on travel tips, cruises, and exotic cooking classes in destination spots. This motivates each employee to stay current (because they know customers will call with questions about the articles), and it enables employees to field frequently asked questions from customers without handing the caller off to someone else in the office.

When managing a rush of calls regarding recent publicity, the person in charge of public relations needs to periodically check with those answering the phones. He or she may find that they are being asked questions they can't answer or that there is some problem that was not anticipated.

Impact Of Poor Internal Branding Effort

Communicating the story to employees never quite gets done in most organizations. How often do you encounter a receptionist who does not know much about what the organization does?

There is another benefit to working on internal branding. When members of the organization have the opportunity to present, they are more likely to engage in what they are doing and to stay current in their professions.

This was driven home to me recently when I noticed that a friend (who rarely reads anything) was reading a professional textbook in preparation for a talk she was doing in a few weeks.

Unfortunately, the most difficult things to measure are often the things that are most important. How much business is lost when the vice president of sales doesn't really understand how the product works or exactly how it is used in the customer's operation? How demotivating is it for a receptionist to work in an organization that can't describe what it does?

Why does this ignorance occur? In most cases it is either because the internal communication is poor or because employees don't take advantage of every opportunity to ask questions and learn more about the product and the field. I believe in most organizations this is the single most ignored part of the business. This is because what can't be measured doesn't get done.

Chapter 15

Execution

The fifth dimension of a marketing infrastructure is execution. It includes things like sales, sales-force management, promotional strategies, and distribution chain management. It is often referred to as "blocking and tackling."

Execution is more important than strategy. Two organizations lack a killer strategy, but one (as the story below will show) succeeds with good execution.

As we discussed before, good strategy without effective implementation will never work, but good implementation can be successful with a mediocre strategy. This is good news for most organizations.

A Tale of Two Companies

The first case study illustrates how a mediocre strategy with good implementation succeeded. The second story shows how a mediocre strategy, with poor execution (at every turn), never got off the ground. Both organizations provide professional education programs.

SCENARIO 1 – SUPERIOR EXECUTION

Few organizations can create a killer strategy like Dell or Southwest Airlines. Fortunately, a well-executed strategy can provide a profitable business despite a less-than-stellar strategy. Here's one story. In 1988, I read an article in the *Cincinnati Business Courier* indicating the dean of the business college, Dan Geeding, wanted to expand the reach of the Center for Management. At the time, the center's product consisted of a public seminar series featuring about thirty seminars offered twice a year. The public seminars generated about $350 thousand per year.

Xavier's brand in the business community was its expertise in management development. That became the basis for all of the programs we developed.

Here are some of the critical steps taken:

1. We set up a front office process which included developing a lead system, a proposal process, a sales and sales funnel management system, and direct marketing.

2. To develop leads, I conducted customer satisfaction surveys after each seminar. This involved contacting about five hundred supervisors, managers, and executives per year.

3. About 20 percent of the participants I contacted, identified another project for us and arranged a meeting with the leadership to discuss the project.

4. The phone surveys also uncovered funding for two other products. This led to products specifically designed for midsize and Fortune 500 and Fortune 1000 companies.

As a result, we doubled revenue within a year and tripled revenue in year two.

Scenario 2 – Execution Gone Haywire

An international professional trade association headquartered in Europe decides to capture the U.S. market for marketing professional services. Its unique strength is a program aimed at the chief marketing officers (CMOs) in professional services firms. Other programs are aimed at directors of marketing and business development managers.

In addition, members are entitled to a monthly magazine, an online biweekly newsletter, web seminars, and access to a database of over one thousand articles.

The strategy for penetrating the U.S. market consists of sponsoring quarterly educational events in key states as a membership enrollment mechanism. This makes sense. I knew from conducting focus groups of American Marketing Association members while serving as the president of a local chapter that this was widely regarded as the most valuable aspect of membership.

To coordinate it, they enroll small business consultants to be regional directors in six East Coast and Midwest states. The regional director is responsible for tapping current members to serve as board members and for arranging a quarterly educational program on a hot marketing topic.

The association also hires a business development manager. His role is to contact participants of these quarterly events to see if they are interested in joining.

There are a number of problems with the execution. They are:

1. Pricing. The association tripled the cost of membership within a few months of its entry in the U.S. market. This made membership three times higher than other, similar associations.

2. Promotion. It took six months longer than anticipated to develop a comprehensive list of potential members. Because compiling the list took so long, invitations to educational events were sent out late. This impacted attendance.

3. Buyer profile. Most of the decision makers for these services were marketing directors with small budgets. To add to the problem, they were not eligible to participate in their best program, which was aimed at chief marketing officers.

4. Staff. The founder of the association had a bad habit of putting inexperienced people in management positions. As a result, every single policy changed within the first four months.

5. Influencers. The regional directors were in the best position to influence. Instead, the association flew a young, inexperienced business development manager to every event to meet and greet potential members. His hard-hitting sales style turned off potential members.

6. Policy. The association decided that event participants must decide whether they wanted to join after the first educational event. If they declined, they could not attend another event.

FAULTY ASSUMPTIONS

In his book *The Marketing Imagination*, Theodore Levitt says, "Most commonly wrong decisions are based on miscalculations or just plain dumb assumptions about the market place – that sales would be sufficiently good, prices sufficiently high, accounts receivable sufficiently low and short term. Hence fiscal failure originates in the market place." [12]

You'll notice that the association made a number of assumptions based on faulty thinking. For instance, well-respected research in books like *Just Ask a Woman* by Mary Lou Quinlan shows that women generally are methodical decision makers, yet the association expected potential members (mostly women) to make a decision based on one event. [13]

Anyone who regularly attends local association meetings knows that the quality of a program can vary dramatically from meeting to meeting. It's unlikely someone will join based on one good program.

More fundamentally, in many markets only a small number of firms have a Chief Marketing Officer. This is significant because most potential members did not qualify for inclusion in the association's signature CMO program.

As a result, the pricing strategy was at odds with the profile of the buyer of the services. Anecdotal data also suggests that marketing directors in professional service firms have tight budgets and usually don't like to purchase anything that might make waves.

In contrast, Xavier's public programs proved to be an excellent method for developing leads. Although the public seminars were not designed to attract the CEO, the participants I contacted were frequently able to identify a key challenge in their organization and arrange a meeting with the CEO to discuss what we could do for them.

The contrasting stories also serve as a good example of the difference between being sales-driven and marketing-driven. Although Xavier charged a fee for the public programs, participants were pleasantly surprised by the quality of the learning experience and the opportunity to network with peers. This created a deep connection with the participants.

PART THREE

CREATING THE RIGHT LAUNCHING PAD (CHAPTERS 16-23)

In this section, we will cover, in more depth, the key activities in a small business that work hand in glove with the marketing infrastructure. This includes concrete steps you can take if you don't have enough customers to establish a dialogue and simple ways to dramatically improve sales results.

We will begin by exploring the key reason some small businesses self-destruct and what you can do to inoculate your organization from this kind of scenario. Small-business owners work hard to cultivate customers, and then—just as the business is growing—their worst instincts can take over. Instituting a simple set of organizing principles will go a long way to ensure that this doesn't happen to you.

Just as you can get a flywheel effect based on the dynamic relationship between developing dialogues with customers and uncovering a niche market, instituting a set of organizing principles reinforces all the elements of the marketing infrastructure. This frees you to work on growing your business.

In addition to also exploring topics such as new trends in marketing and how to avoid the universal tendency to take customers for granted, we will finish with the latest research on creating the results you want.

CHAPTER 16

WHY SMALL BUSINESSES SELF-DESTRUCT

Many small business owners unwittingly get in the way of their own success. Usually it is because they are furiously protective of their customers or fail to get in the shoes of the other people they interact with on a regular basis. This can alienate employees (particularly salespeople), consultants, suppliers, and even some customers. As a result, some small business owners drive away the very people they will need to create an effective marketing infrastructure.

> *Organizations are frequently successful in the short run, but will later derail (or limp along indefinitely) due to a fundamental lack of effective relationships with customers and/or other stakeholders.*

SCENARIO 1

A few years ago, I met a small business owner that was in the 'mystery shopping' market. I was interested in working with him. After several meetings, I attended his half-day seminar.

A week later, I met his partner at a networking event by accident (I was not aware he had a partner). This, of course, changed everything. It meant both partners had to buy into every issue that came up in the business and share the profits. This didn't look like a win for me. More fundamentally, I no longer trusted the owner.

SCENARIO 2

I met with the two owners of a small consulting business (who, by the way, both had very hot cars parked in front of their offices). They told me their business was out of touch with their customers. They wanted me to conduct a customer satisfaction survey.

They assured me that their customers were satisfied. I assured them that if most customers were satisfied, they could expect almost 20 percent would have a new project.

After getting agreement on project scope and cost, they began to add a host of other things they wanted (beyond the scope of the project). It was clear they were trying to get as much as possible for as little as possible.

WHAT HAPPENED?

In both cases the small-business owners were only thinking about the exchange from their perspectives.

These kinds of experiences don't happen as frequently when you are working for a small division of a larger organization, because the larger organization provides many of the resources needed. This is unique to small businesses with few resources.

THE SALESPERSON IS THE ENEMY

Another frequent dynamic is that the salesperson is viewed as the enemy.

In order to be effective, salespeople need to build on a base of goodwill, such as referrals and current and past customers. If you don't give the salesperson an opportunity to create a flywheel effect from referrals and customers, it is difficult to create any momentum. Here are some key reasons the job of selling is hard in a small business:

1. Consumers are faced with an overwhelming number of choices; there is a lot of noise. It is difficult to get the attention of C-level executives.

2. Small businesses often do not have effective phone scripts, success stories, testimonials, or brochures.

3. Small businesses often don't have a lot of insight into such things as the profile of their ideal prospects.

4. Small businesses don't have much bandwidth. The salesperson may need to get involved in some aspect of delivery, which takes away from selling time (and commission income).

CLONING EFFECTIVE SALESPEOPLE

Scott Jacobs of Harvest Consulting LLC points out that a lot of small-business owners are individuals that have technical knowledge in some aspect of business. This enables them to be successful at selling, but they may have difficultly finding someone who has the same level of subject matter knowledge.

There is a related problem. Small businesses don't have the resources to develop essential sales tools. The owner of the business is able to quickly recall several success stories that are applicable in specific sales situations, but the salesperson may not have the history with the organization to do that.

While it is true that the salesperson can work with the owner to develop these stories, the owner often doesn't see the value of doing this. The owner has been successful due to things like contacts in the industry and personal credibility. She often doesn't realize the salesperson is not working from the same baseline.

Why Sales Is The Enemy

The salesperson is the enemy because the owner doesn't want to pay a commission to develop new business from current customers. It stems from the delusional belief that customers will call when they have a need.

Creating A Win-Win Situation

Jack owns a small consulting firm. He wants to generate $1 million in revenue, but for the last year, he increasingly has been selling primarily to entrepreneurs and small businesses.

I knew from conversations with some of his customers he was leaving lots of money on the table by not touching base with his past midsize customers, but he resists the idea of having his salesperson contact his database of customers.

The reason is simple. Jack calculates his fees on a cost-plus basis. Because his fee structure does not provide the profit he needs, he nickel-and-dimes clients by charging extra for faxes and phone calls. This, of course, makes customers mad. They delay payment by at least a few months and then select a competitor the next time they have a marketing project.

The reality is that his services have a lot of value to a midsize firm, but C-level executives don't want to invest in suppliers who may go out of business. They want suppliers who know how to price (although they may occasionally need to be reminded of this). As a result of this miscalculation, Jack isn't getting paid on time and he can't afford to pay a commission. Furthermore, his marketing materials screamed "competent, cheap marketing services," which, of course, appeals to entrepreneurs.

How We Tripled Revenue

1. Jack redesigned his marketing communications and methodology to appeal to midsize clients.

2. We began pricing on a project basis. This increased the fee 30 percent.

3. He won substantial contracts from several midsize companies within a month.

4. Jack could then justify the cost of a commission. The salesperson developed new business from about 20 percent of his current customer base and added several sizable, new national accounts.

Think Like A Big Company

Christine Wright, proprietor of Customer Insights, Inc., says, "Small-business owners need to think more like large businesses." When Jack realized he had the capabilities to help midsize businesses (with some small inexpensive changes to his business) he tripled revenue.

Beyond that, there are some specific ways that you can structure the business to avoid the trap of creating the kind of reactionary environment that leads to self-sabotage. We will cover this in the next chapter

Chapter 17

Getting Everyone On The Same Page

A short set of simple organizing, or operating, principles serves as a compass for everyone in an organization. The operating principles are: policy, value exchange, and allocation of resources.

When an organization fails to have a coherent approach to execution or when the business owner is making decisions that compromise relationships, one or more of these principles are usually involved.

> *A set of organizing principles keeps everyone honest. It is an antidote to the kind of reactive environment that can result when a small-business owner has not established a set of principles that reflect his or her best instincts.*

Policy

Most organizations are unaware of how powerful policies are. Policies inform every action in an organization. For instance, in 1986, Dun & Bradstreet had a policy of not providing customers with monthly statements. When some of the salespeople in the Cincinnati office started misrepresenting how many units of information the customer had purchased in order to sell more units, I considered talking to a high level executive at headquarters. Ultimately, I left instead.

I realized that by having a policy of not providing customers a statement detailing monthly usage, Dun & Bradstreet was winking at the salespeople and opening the door to abuse.

For the first forty years, a manufacturer of high quality tools for contractors focused on quality. But, as "big box" retailers entered the market, two things happened: foreign competitors were able to produce the same level of quality for less and "big box" retailers were squeezing their profit margins.

The leadership realized they needed to develop innovative new-to-the-world products that were not easily duplicated. At the same time, they had a policy of repairing any tool a customer sent back. This was a time-consuming task that left employees confused and left little space for creating new-to-the-world product ideas.

Recognizing the mixed messages they were sending, they decided to make producing innovative products the cornerstone of their business. To do this, the leadership literally had to go back to school to figure out how to create an innovative environment. This was a dramatic shift for a group of leaders used to managing based solely on experience. In the third year of the innovation initiative, the company developed fifty-five new products.

Value Exchange

Business is based on value exchanges, yet many organizations consistently fail to get on the other side of the desk and look at offerings from the customer's perspective.

> *It starts with customers, but the concept of a value exchange must run deeper than just customers. It's an ethic that permeates every kind of exchange. If you don't treat everyone with respect, your relationship with customers will ultimately suffer.*

The professional association profiled in the chapter entitled "Execution" failed this test in every aspect of implementation. In addition to having a weak value proposition, they were never able to get into the shoes of the regional directors who were key stakeholders in making the expansion into the U.S. market work. In contrast, Xavier was able to capitalize on a priceless experience that led to the development of new business and profitable new products.

Allocation of Resources

In his book *The Marketing Edge*, Thomas Bonoma makes a convincing argument (based on his own research) that when organizations try to excel in all aspects of marketing execution, they end up suboptimizing on all fronts. [14] In other words, you don't need to add advertising to the mix if other forms of promotion are producing the results you want.

Because many businesses think they must include all forms of promotion, they rationalize things like poor trade show results by insisting that if they didn't show up customers and prospects would wonder why.

A better way to think about poor results is to question whether it makes sense to engage in a poorly performing promotional activity. You want to leverage promotional efforts that yield the best results (See the appendix for a more detailed exploration of trade shows).

Execution Strategy Drivers

Execution is critical to managing scarce resources. It requires seeing the nuances of every action you take. In a nutshell, your strategy, your execution competencies, and your selling process must be linked.

The consulting firm profiled earlier is a good example. Recall that they decided to focus on the hospital market. Their reasons were as follows: their product worked with overwhelmed executives, C-level executives were accessible at conferences, and they excelled at making presentations.

There are three important driving forces in getting the right execution strategy. They are: goals, relationship capacity, and assumptions.

GOALS

Organizations get into trouble when goals and actions are not in sync. If actions don't match goals, they are counterproductive. You'll recall that the small-business owner, Jack, spent most of his time courting entrepreneurs. This was inconsistent with his ambitious revenue goal.

Another common problem in underperforming organizations is that they fail to act even when they know what they need to do. An educational foundation has been told over and over by prospective customers that it needs to develop a success story. A national professional association knows it needs to find out what members are thinking. Both fail to act for more than four years.

RELATIONSHIP CAPACITY

To have a true relationship with a customer, your product must solve a key pain. Short of that, you are simply another vendor. Let's look at two situations that illuminate the difference.

If your product does solve a key pain, then you must develop a credible mechanism for reaching the key decision maker. That mechanism must be based on something you do well. For instance, at Xavier, we leveraged our seminar series to get to the key C-level decision maker.

Senco, on the other had, has a vendor relationship with "big box" retailers. Senco realizes that it must improve the product itself in order to improve its standing with both the customer and "big box" retailers. To do that, the leadership must focus on creating innovative products.

ASSUMPTIONS

Faulty assumptions are often based on a lack of a dialogue with customers, but sometimes it's more fundamental. It occurs when a business doesn't consider the entire context.

For instance, a retail tire chain decides to improve its value proposition by offering nitrogen-filled tires. I'm told that this type of tire is used in race cars to hold air pressure. I purchase these tires but find that my tires still need air added from time to time. My car dealership, local lube retail chain, and my emergency road service all claim that they cannot fill my tires. They either regard it as dangerous or they don't have the equipment.

This means I must return to the retail chain that sold the tires when my tires look low. Perhaps this was part of their strategy, but after experiencing this inconvenience, one of my key criteria for purchasing new tires was—you guessed it— a retail tire store that does not sell nitrogen-filled tires.

AN EXECUTION-CHALLENGED BUSINESS

Some businesses are really difficult to promote. A few years ago, a friend of mine wanted to test the feasibility of offering a national telemarketing program to Mail Boxes, Etc. franchises (it is now known as The UPS Store). It was not a very desirable approach to promotion, but I was interested in the concept of devising a national telemarketing program. I reluctantly offered to help him prototype it with two stores.

The small-business owner thought large corporations were the key market for his services in the downtown business district, but we discovered his best customers were small, growing professional services firms looking to outsource administrative work (such as the packaging of proposals, sales presentations, and trade show exhibits). Because he was able to dramatically enhance the appearance of customers' documents, he improved his customers chances of getting sales and saved each of the businesses the cost of an administrative assistant.

Instead of getting an unpredictable amount of small projects from large businesses (on short notice), each professional services client he acquired generated a predictable $20 thousand per year. This enabled him to develop a few "back-of-the-envelope" numbers to predict revenue and run the business.

> *This story also demonstrates, once again, that uncovering a market segment or niche that values your offerings is an efficient way to uncover what you can do better than anyone else.*

CHAPTER 17

END-OF-THE-CHAPTER QUESTIONS

1. What policies drive your business?

2. How can you (or do you) instill the concept of consistently creating value exchanges in your organization?

Chapter 18

Selling – The Ultimate Test Of Execution

The specialized knowledge you have developed by focusing on one market puts you at a distinct advantage over competitors, but you still need to be relentless in continuously improving the sales process.

Each customer needs to be evaluated at both the strategic and the tactical level.

What's Your Customer's Risk Profile?

> *Most C-level executives are operating on two levels. They are looking for something new and they are adverse to risk.*

You may observe this during a sales call. Early in conversation, the C-level executive may have a lot of energy around solving a challenge, but as the conversation progresses (and a solution emerges) he or she may begin to surface concerns.

They have arrived at a point where they must assume risk in order to move forward. Few people like change (which is really what you are asking them to do).

The Three Risk Profiles

Your products are designed to attract a certain type of customer. Most executives fall into one of three risk profiles. They are innovators, problem solvers, or reactives. All three will respond in very different ways to your product offerings. Here is a brief snapshot of the three profiles:

Innovators

Innovators are willing to go for broke. They are looking for a solution that will enable them to leapfrog over competitors on some critical dimension of their business.

This usually involves solving a previously unsolvable problem in their industry or it may involve applying technology to achieve some competitive advantage. It often requires co-creating a new-to-the-world product with a supplier who has a unique set of competencies.

Problem Solvers

Problem solvers genuinely want to succeed, but are conservative by nature. Timing is critical with problem solvers. Once they uncover the root cause of some obstacle in their business, they are open about their situation and are willing to explore a variety of options.

They are looking for a supplier who has a whole-product solution. Because they are more conservative than innovators, you may need to do a pilot first.

Reactives

Reactives purchase only after it becomes painfully obvious that their current solution is not sufficient. They are frustrating to work with because the leader often does not want to solve the fundamental issues in the business.

The members of a reactive organization require lots of emotional support. They are conflicted between the need to address long-standing problems and the desire to make the problems go away. They tend to be perfectionistic in orientation. Consequently, when working with the leader of a reactive organization (and his or her team), you must be prepared to provide an in-depth overview of the issues and back up recommendations with concrete proof.

For instance, if I am conducting a customer survey, I will meet regularly with the leadership to review the data (and its implications). This will fully prepare them to make strategic decisions about the future direction of the business.

WHICH CUSTOMER RISK PROFILE DO YOU ATTRACT?

One of the chief differences between the various risk profiles is how they respond to a challenge. Innovators proactively look for ways to improve performance. Reactives are on the other end of the spectrum. They may spend years in denial before they are willing to acknowledge a problem. With both problem solvers and reactives, timing is critical. They will not buy until they have given a good deal of thought to exactly how they need to solve a problem.

In the lifetime of your business, you may oscillate between all three types of customers. For instance, if you create a new product that solves the limitations of current offerings, it is possible to move from working mainly with reactives to working with either innovators or problem solvers. On the other hand, the more your product consists of a set of tried-and-true lock-step product components that require little imagination from the customer, the more it will be attractive to reactives.

CAN YOU REALLY ADDRESS THE PROBLEM?

There are three things to consider in answering this question. They are: Do you have a whole-product solution? Are you able to customize your product? and How does your product impact customers' processes? Let's look at each question.

Do You Have A Whole-Product Solution?

To answer this question, ask yourself what happens once your work is complete. Will the customer need to purchase something else to get to the next step? Providing everything a customer will need to solve a problem improves your chances of winning business.

Let me give you a simple example. I have a leak in my roof. Several roofers tell me that I need a new roof. A third roofer (who also specializes in chimneys) tells me that I also need a new crown on my chimney. If I conclude that he is right, I am more likely to have him do both projects because there are things he will do in completing the chimney project that might be duplicated if I hire someone else to do the roof.

If you don't offer a whole-product solution, does your product work in conjunction with other products? For instance, if you offer sales training, you may design your program to mesh with the leading personality assessment instruments in the industry.

If you don't have a whole-product solution (and it's not possible to embed the other elements you might need), is there a way to redesign your product so that the customer does not need to purchase something else?

For instance, many organizations that contract with a customer research company want to know what their customers are thinking, and they want to do a market segmentation study to figure out where they should focus their energies. My approach addresses all these issues by using the customer data from the surveys to identify a niche strategy.

Are You Able To Customize Your Product?

Can your product be customized to meet a variety of situations? This may appear to be similar to being able to design a solution by starting with a blank page, but it is actually different. When conducting phone surveys or sales calls, the customer will offer an overwhelming amount of detail. Having a mental model of all of the ways in which the product can be configured is useful.

For instance, an executive coaching firm may specialize in working exclusively with executive teams or it may offer specialized programs to executive teams, high potential leaders, managers, and supervisors.

If the organization only works with executive teams, it will still diagnose situations by starting with a blank page, but it will likely have a standard methodology in the actual delivery. Someone who offers programs to several different groups will likely have a different approach for each group (even though their content is drawn from the same source).

How Does Your Product Impact Customers' Processes?

If your products require the customer to change or eliminate an internal business process, the selling process will be much harder. In his book *The Marketing Edge,* Bonoma found that even if you can show an organization conclusive proof that a new product or service will save money, the organization will be unlikely to buy if it means changing a core business process.[15]

This has also been documented by Stanford professor Robert Sutton in his book *Weird Ideas That Work*. In fact, the care and feeding of current business processes is a key reason it is difficult for businesses to innovate.[16]

What You Need To Bring To The Table

As the earlier story of Rob's efforts to win another consulting contract shows, what you bring to the table is just as important as your actual conversation with the customer. There are three essential elements to success. They are: credibility, precall preparation, and timing.

Credibility

Recall that Rob had difficulty getting the prospect to provide any information. The problem was that although Rob was thoroughly prepared, he did not establish credibility. It is essential to the selling process. There are three types of credibility. They are: personal credibility, product credibility, and organizational credibility.

1. Personal Credibility. This is established by the salesperson's knowledge of the product and its application to a customer's business. Being articulate about the value proposition, being able to reference applicable success stories, and serving in leadership roles in the industry are all examples of ways to establish this type of credibility.

2. Product Credibility. This is achieved by being successful in solving tough problems and gaining endorsements from customers and Industry Influencers. Specializing in one market segment (or niche) makes it easier to do that.

3. Organizational Credibility. Organizational credibility is based on your reputation in the market, your values, your financial strength, and how well you stand behind your products.

PRECALL PREPARATION

Establishing personal credibility starts with learning as much about an organization as possible before making a sales call. Acquiring this knowledge involves things like studying the prospect's website, reading articles about the business, and talking to employees, customers, and suppliers.

If they are already a customer, it's important not to make assumptions about their current situation based on past experience. If your customer is facing a difficult environment, the customer will be influenced by outside consultants and by its own key customers.

Engaging in this type of due diligence enables the salesperson to know exactly how to approach the conversation.

We see the same process employed by job candidates. I recall reading about the selection of Marvin Lewis as head coach of the Cincinnati Bengal organization. In the interview, Lewis talked about his vision for the team and the specific tactical moves he planned to use to win. He also made it clear he was in charge of all the key decisions and the public image of the organization (an indication that he understood what had hampered the team's effectiveness in the past).

Timing

If you correctly diagnose a key pain in an organization and the organization is keenly aware it has a problem, you may succeed in gaining a sale by simply being there at exactly the right time with the right solution. In this situation, timing will trump credibility.

On the other hand, if you correctly diagnose the problem, but the prospect is not quite ready to admit a problem exists, a sale is not possible. The customer must acknowledge a problem or improvement issue before a sale can occur. This is a long process if the organization is risk adverse. The leadership must struggle with the pain until they are willing to confront the reality of their situation.

Once an organization is tired of complaining and finger-pointing, it will begin to engage in uncovering the true reasons for its problems. The diagnoses may be off the mark, but the timing is right for a sale.

Your Sales Process

Because selling and the selling process are both critical to reaping the benefits of a marketing infrastructure, reviewing your selling process can pay real dividends.

Elements of the Sales Process

1. The face-to-face communication process. It doesn't matter which book you use (*Solution Selling*, *Spin Selling*, etc.). What's important is to have a common, disciplined approach to selling.

2. The process for negotiating the various buying influences. *Strategic Selling* is the bible for managing the politics of each selling situation.

3. Your internal process for moving the sale to a conclusion (this includes things like events, presentations, pilots, etc.).

4. The prospect's evaluation process. The salesperson must mesh the seller's selling process with the buyer's evaluation process.

ANALYZING THE SELLING PROCESS

1. What objections does sales typically encounter in each phase of the selling process? Are there better ways to address them? Where are the stumbling blocks in the sales process? For instance, does sales agree to an initial meeting without the key C-level decision-maker present?

2. How can you revise the sales process in light of new insights? One approach is to work with your team to devise a detailed map of each element of the sales process, such as the key objectives, questions, and responses.

    Consultants, such as Pam Beigh of SALESCORE, can assist you. Her website success stories will convince you that doing this exercise is worth your time.

OTHER RECOMMENDATIONS

1. The proposal process should be developed from a standard template. The summary statement (in the beginning) should be personalized to clearly describe the situation and show how your product will solve the problem (Everything you write should reflect what the buyer and seller agreed on at the conclusion of the last meeting).

2. Use weekly sales meetings to discuss strategies for closing a particular sale. For instance, if you use the book *Strategic Selling* to manage the influences in a selling process (such as the Economic Buyer, User Buyer, etc), you can brainstorm how to reach a key influencer. This discipline helps everyone be more effective in thinking through the sales process.

3. Meet on a quarterly basis (at least) to track the sales funnel and estimate revenue. The sales funnel will also help you gauge revenue projections for the top of the funnel, the middle of the funnel, and the end of the funnel.

4. Work with your best performer. That person can be invaluable in deciphering the most effective approach to selling.

TACTICAL MARKETING

In a small business, a salesperson must be a marketer as well as a salesperson. Salespeople often don't act off a formal marketing plan. They work at an intuitive level by looking at the actions they can take today to support the sales process. Here are some examples:

1. Creating a database of customers and prospects.

2. Conducting customer satisfaction surveys to develop more business opportunities.

3. Sending out a short e-mail newsletter with valuable tips to customers and prospects.

4. Being an active participant in a local or national professional association.

5. Developing a blog.

Rich Bitting, a sales and marketing consultant, agrees that these activities are a critical part of generating business. He advises, "Exercise care not to overwhelm the prospect with too frequent communications. Use as many marketing channels as appropriate to your particular client base and use them judiciously.

The goal is to engage your customer base in a manner that they will look forward to your communications. Educate them with measured bits of useful information or entertain them with related news and events along with your marketing message. Give them a positive reason to remember your brand."

Chapter 18

End-Of-The-Chapter Questions

You may want to involve your team in answering these questions:

1. What is your organization's process for preparing for an initial sales meeting with a prospect or current customer? How might you improve on this process?

2. What is the biggest objection prospects routinely make that can't be answered?

3. Looking back at some successful sales situations, what was the motivating factor (or factors) that led to a successful close?

Chapter 19

The Care And Feeding Of Customers

There is always a conflict between what you are able to deliver and all the things the customer wants you to do. To appropriately deal with this, it's useful to develop a perspective on what makes customers tick.

Customers Are Different

To begin with, each customer has a unique set of business processes, competitive conditions, and motivations. Consequently, all customers develop a distinctive point of view, but they may also share some prevalent bias of their industry. All of these influences mean you may need to show how your product can solve what prospective customers may have written off as an unsolvable problem.

For instance, several attorneys run a legal outsourcing firm that enables a small firm to outsource legal work that is not very profitable. Unfortunately, some solo practitioners lack the business savvy to see how this will free them to generate more business from more profitable parts of their business. They have accepted the status quo.

Although the two owners of the legal outsourcing firm have developed a business head, they must get into the shoes of their less savvy customers in order to continue to win business from sole practitioners.

> *Articulating your value proposition in a way that customers and prospects can relate to is the key communication challenge of any intangible product.*

Once you have mastered this communication challenge and have successfully negotiated a sale, the real work of carving out an effective relationship begins.

Common Barriers To Customer Satisfaction

Here are some common ways that your relationship to the customer can derail. The first one may surprise you.

Taking Customers For Granted

All organizations take customers for granted. This is not a subject we talk about very much, but there is a natural tendency in all organizations to do this. This has implications for the kinds of dialogues we have (or don't have) with customers.

How often does something like this happen to you? A professional association offers each new member a free lunch. Meanwhile, though you have been a loyal member for seven years, you are expected to pay for the monthly luncheon. Organizations send this type of message to their customers all the time.

Operating At The Wrong Scale

Companies are frequently preoccupied with internal needs rather than the needs of the customer. If an organization lacks a marketing infrastructure, all of its marketing efforts are occurring at the wrong scale. Consequently, the business has no hope of ever connecting with customers.

In an informal discussion with six directors of marketing in the professional services market, I learned how they spent most of their time. It consisted of things like assisting in creating sales presentations; improving marketing communications, and developing new business.

Because they don't have the information they need to develop anything but a superficial perspective on their own organization and their customers, their marketing activities will fail to illuminate what their business can do better than anyone else.

Lack Of Follow Up

In many organizations, once the sale is concluded, the seller moves on and it's up to the customer to make sure the purchase achieves the promised results. If the customer is dissatisfied, it's not long before he or she realizes that the salesperson left as soon as they "got ink" and will never return.

If an organization is selling a single product there is no way to know with certainty if further efforts by the salesperson will pay off. Additional efforts by the salesperson also reduces the time spent acquiring new customers.

Even organizations that have opportunities to cross-sell are often reluctant to conduct customer surveys. This is frequently because they don't know how to engage the customer in a dialogue and they fear a customer satisfaction survey may open Pandora's box.

Disputes Around Ownership

In the professional services arena, the consultant or attorney who develops a new account often delivers the service. If the organization is sales-driven, this individual will view the client as his or her customer and will likely resist the involvement of other experts in the firm. This extends to any contact with the client.

The marketing department often throws gasoline on the fire by insisting on conducting a customer satisfaction survey. This is not the best place to start (it's too threatening). A benchmark study is a better starting point because it's the best way to uncover the client's key challenge without compromising the individual who delivered the service.

If marketing is unable to initiate some sort of dialogue, the firm's value proposition is gradually diminished due to the lack of a mechanism for making the connection between the firm's offerings and clients' challenges.

Managing "After-The-Sale" Expectations

Once you have successfully sold something, the clock is ticking. Customers will make lots of demands and expect results. The circumstances of the customer's business may make delivery difficult, but the customer will still expect you to provide the value you promised.

From Satisfied To Disgruntled

Here are the typical phases all customers go through without the benefit of an effective intervention.

Phase 1: The Honeymoon

Once your organization begins working with a customer, the customer will have complaints. This is good. He or she is invested in your solution (This is also why customer satisfaction actually goes up when a customer complains and the seller responds).

Phase 2: A Problem Surfaces

In many cases, the first sign of trouble is a call to the salesperson. The customer wants to find ways to improve the current performance of a product or service. He or she wants the salesperson to be involved in a group discussion regarding this issue.

The meeting will involve an executive and the customers actually using the product. Even if your organization will not be conducting the meeting, it is critical that the salesperson understands how to lead a group in problem solving. They will need to provide input if the session is not structured in a way that will lead to a solution (there are a number of educational institutions that offer training in facilitation).

If this type of facilitated problem-solving situation is uncomfortable, members of your organization may avoid this type of showdown or fail to get the problem resolved in a satisfactory way.

A pre-meeting discussion between the salesperson, the customer, and perhaps others in your organization is the first order of business. It can be done by phone. The goal is to determine what options exist for an acceptable solution. This will enable your organization to be prepared to talk about what your organization is doing to address the sources of dissatisfaction during the customer-initiated meeting.

This can be an intimidating process, but non-participation is not an option if the organization wants to maintain a relationship with the account. Providing a process and training will empower the salesperson to deal with the situation.

PHASE 3: THE END GAME

If Phase 2 is not successfully negotiated, the customer believes he or she can do better elsewhere. The customer no longer complains because he or she is no longer invested.

> *Because the customer is no longer complaining, the organization may assume that the problem blew over. There were complaints in the beginning, but now it appears the customer is satisfied. The opposite is true. The customer is actively looking for another solution.*

COUNTERING CUSTOMER INDIFFERENCE BY DESIGN

Gus, the owner of Gus Perdikakis Associates Inc. goes the extra mile to avoid the trap of taking customers for granted. His motto is "I want the customer to come to me if there is a problem and I want the customer to tell everyone they know if they are happy." He does this by anticipating sources of customer dissatisfaction before it occurs.

His company provides contract technical experts in markets such as consumer packaged goods, energy, and manufacturing. They are available for a variety of assignments lasting from as short as a few weeks to several months or even years.

Through trial and error, here's what they do to be customer centered:

1. They go to school on their customers by specializing in a few markets that require similar technical competencies.

2. They break down the customer's needs into three categories: technical skills, logistics, and soft skills. Gus found this is the best way to uncover other requirements.

3. They take their contract employees to lunch in order to anticipate problems and to give their contract employees a heads-up when something in the client's organization has changed.

4. If a contract employee is not working out, Gus does an intervention. The contract employee, the employee's boss, and Gus meet to look at ways to resolve the problem (and deal with the negatives).

5. Gus also provides ongoing technical training in hot new areas of technology.

This process may appear to be obvious, but it's based on observing how things went wrong and taking corrective actions. A sign that this is not occurring is when a business makes excuses. If a business does not have processes designed to create a stellar customer experience, it's not happening.

Strategies For Valuing Customers

One of the ways an organization can combat the natural tendency to take customers for granted (and improve the customer experience) is to create internal educational experiences. Here are some examples:

Provide A Platform For Teams To Share Customer Stories

Provide lunch once a week and have teams volunteer to talk about things like working directly with a customer to solve a problem, observing customers using your product, or successfully selling a piece of business.

Help Front-Line People Be More Effective

Work with the customer service team to identify the kinds of questions and problems they have difficulty answering (if your time is limited, there are consultants who can provide this service). Ask each team member to keep a diary of other questions and problems that pop up.

Meet every few weeks to compare notes and discuss better ways to resolve these questions and problems. This is also an opportunity to address customer issues that cannot be solved by customer service.

Share Customer Data With Everyone

I find that even busy people make time to meet (even weekly) to learn more about what customers are thinking. These meetings can include things like a presentation detailing the results of a recent phone survey of customers or a briefing from the salespeople about what they are learning in the field.

Bring Customers To The Office

When you bring customers to the office, the whole organization has new energy. This kind of informal interaction also encourages an organization to think about its marketing message. You want everyone in the organization to be able to articulate in a clear and compelling way what your organization does.

When A Project Fails

Despite your best efforts, sometimes customers cannot be satisfied and they leave. Most organizations view these situations as being beyond their control, but the manager directly involved in using your product can be invaluable in learning why a project failed. Most organizations don't take advantage of this opportunity.

> *Any failure is a chance to make giant leaps in learning. It doesn't matter if you executed perfectly and it was all the customer's fault; you may learn something you can do to dramatically improve results in the future.*

Here's an actual situation from my own experience: A client decided to switch to a competitor. Later we learned from ongoing conversations with the manager in charge of implementing our program, that Design Engineers were not always the key gatekeeper in selling situations. All of our marketing campaigns had been designed around that faulty assumption.

As a result of this information, we realized that a monthly meeting with the customer's sales team would have uncovered the problem.

It's The Customer

When the customer is resistant to an approach, addressing it from another scale can work. For instance, if a customer is concerned that a campaign won't work, pilot it with the top salespeople before involving the entire sales force.

There are, however, situations in which you must end a customer relationship. Some businesses have a culture of making unreasonable demands as a way of doing business.

How Smart Small Businesses Grow

When customers make demands that tax your business to the point that their service expectations exceed the profit you need to make, it's time to end the relationship in the most tactful way possible. One way consultants do this is to politely explain that the project the client has in mind is not something they enjoy doing. Most customers can understand this response.

Chapter 19

End-Of-The-Chapter Questions

1. What processes do you have in place for managing customer satisfaction after the sale?

2. How do you reward customers who provide you with more business?

Chapter 20

New Trends In Marketing

A new emphasis on how the customer experiences a product has resulted in some of the most exciting new trends in marketing. We will explore these trends and its implications in this chapter.

Historically, most businesses have put a lot of focus on communicating their value proposition (particularly during the selling process). Only recently have many businesses realized that customers are interested in the entire experience.

In the business-to-business sector, the ability to fit your product into the customer's organization is a key part of what customer's value. In the consumer market, the way a customer uses a product has become a key element of improving the customer's experience. The way a customer experiences a product also depends on the product.

The Way Customers Experience Your Product

Starbucks profoundly changed the perception of coffee (and expanded the appeal of coffee drinks to a younger demographic) by bringing the European coffeehouse experience to the United States. In fact, Starbucks is often cited as the perfect example of the "experience economy".[17] This means that much of the value of what is being offered by a product or service is the experience itself.

The impact of wrapping a product or service around an experience can profoundly change an industry. In the early 1980s, people in their early twenties were drinking soft drinks. Suppliers of coffee, such as Folgers and Maxwell House, believed they were destined to lose market share in the wake of the post-baby boomer generation 'coming of age'. That didn't happen.

It's not at all uncommon to see students as young as those in junior high school hanging out at Starbucks after school. Coffee has become hip. In fact, some of my middle-aged male associates are regulars of a Starbucks frequented by female high school students who wear short skirts. We can deduce from this story that it is unlikely that coffee would have retained its popularity without wrapping it around an experience.

THE PSYCHOLOGY BEHIND EXPERIENCES

To really understand what it's all about, we need to define the ideal elements of a memorable experience. A few years ago, I met with a psychologist from Procter & Gamble who studied ways to create great experiences. I think they were still reeling from the success of Starbucks—after all, P&G invented the tagline "Good to the Last Drop."

He told me that there are six keys to a stellar experience. They are: great food, theme, superior content, fear, surprise, and multiple outcomes. He said that the best examples are Las Vegas and Disney.

I had a hard time getting over his comment about fear until I considered that some of my most unforgettable experiences required me to perform. There is always an aspect of fear in performing (particularly when presenting to a large audience).

I also recalled a situation in which, ironically, P&G sponsored a group of employees from their manufacturing facility for a week-long program at Xavier University. The participants were clearly uncomfortable. Many of them had never taken a class in a university setting and they were required to make presentations. However, at the end of the week, many of the participants said that the experience was one of the highlights of their career. (For more on creating proprietary events see "Events" in the Appendix).

Ease Of Use

The vision of Starbucks is to be the third place we go to seek a welcome respite from our daily routine. It also fits into our lives. It can be a quick stop on the way to work, a destination for a business meeting, or a place for getting work done.

Unlike Starbucks, many consumer products, such as Tide detergent, are difficult to turn into an experience. Consequently, producers of packaged goods must view the experience in a larger context to determine if the nature of the product lends itself to improving the point-of-purchase experience. To do that, they must look at the entire transaction from the consumer's perspective.

For instance, high-quality skin care products, such as the Olay brand of cosmetics, are now available at the local grocery chain. Before this, women often made special trips to retail department stores to purchase one or two cosmetic items. For me, this often entailed spending fifteen minutes searching for a parking space.

Similarly, the experience of using technology products can often be improved by observing the way a customer uses a product. The path to more profitable business for Xerox involved downsizing the overengineered functionality of their products. They found customers wanted something that they could intuitively learn. Customers also didn't want to pay for features they didn't use. Less is more.

Creating A Community Experience

Starbucks has clearly proven that the experience economy is alive and kicking. But what is less understood is the way in which companies like Starbucks and Whole Foods begin by creating a sense of community among their employees. For both organizations, creating a sense of community seems to be an important ingredient in creating a great experience for customers.

Starbucks and Whole Foods go about it in different ways. According to Howard Shultz, founder and CEO of Starbucks, one of the keys for him was to share the success of Starbucks with employees. Even before Starbucks was profitable, they offered health insurance to every employee, including part-time employees.

Whole Foods sees every employee as a team member. The employees provide feedback to each other, rate each other on performance, and share duties. In this sense, employees are working for each other rather than competing with each other for points with a manager. When employees work as a team, the customer picks up the positive vibe. It becomes an integral part of the experience.

We have to consider, though, that this type of atmosphere is not always well received by those who don't fit into the ideal customer profile. In a recent study, Dunkin' Donuts customers were asked to switch with Starbucks customers. One disgruntled Dunkin Donuts customer complained that hanging out at Starbucks was like having Christmas dinner with people you don't know.

You can also create an experience that doesn't start with location. For instance, several years ago, Kroger began making a conscious effort to help students in racially segregated neighborhoods find jobs. Many were also encouraged to apply at Kroger stores throughout the city. As the sons and daughters of parents in the African American community began working in historically all-white neighborhoods, the parents (and grandparents) became more comfortable shopping in the Kroger stores where their children or grandchildren worked.

Just as creating a community among the staff is, according to Shultz, the key to the success of marketing Starbucks, Kroger's success in creating a sense of belonging among an underserved constituency in the Cincinnati community meets its strategic goal of increasing Kroger's market share in the Cincinnati region.

Using Technology To Create A Community

Technology has created new ways to use the concept of community (and collaboration) to generate more business. Here are some ways technology is being harnessed:

Blogs

Blogs can be used to support the concept of community building. For instance, if you're in the software business, the technical buyers for your products are likely sharing information about their experiences with your product on a Blog. Creating a Blog on your website enables you to be in the loop.

Of course, it's easy to have an unhappy customer who will make his or her displeasure known on your Blog. A negative comment about your product will, hopefully, draw out the "quiet advocates" who will defend your product when others offer negative feedback, but this is not a given. For this reason, I don't think a Blog is a no-brainer for every business. My biggest concern is the lack of control.

Similarly, in a speech extolling the virtues of a company-sponsored Blog, the Director of Marketing for an architectural firm added that a Blog was a great way to promote an upcoming event. The problem with that is that controlling who attends an event is critical to avoid being blocked later in the selling process.

Viral Marketing

Viral Marketing is typically used to promote an event or new product. Here's how it works: You ask ten to twenty members of your network (or customers) to send e-mails to at least five people they know. One key is to look for people who have a logical connection. For instance,

Elaine Schneider

if I am speaking, I might tap members of the American Marketing Association.

Rapid Reordering Systems

Kroger collaborates directly with its packaged goods suppliers to find ways to sell more through promotions, displays, product placement, and rapid reordering systems.

Kroger customers present a personalized card at the checkout counter. The card automatically reorders each product the customer purchases. (This reduces the chance another customer will not find a certain item on the shelf). The customer will also save money on specific purchases and may receive coupons based on current and past purchase history. By working collaboratively, Kroger and its suppliers maximize the number of purchases each customer makes while in the store.

Internet Surveys

Internet surveys are becoming the key to creating a community of customers who become part of the sales force (particularly in the consumer market space). The roots of this innovation are found in the death of traditional promotional strategies.

Marketing to consumers is an incredibly difficult process. The only way a cereal company can know its customers is through customer profiling, and to pile it on, traditional one-way promotional strategies are becoming less effective.

One method of engaging the customer is to create an interactive experience. That also nets a small group of advocates who can sway others to buy a particular product.

It can be instructive to learn how this is done. John Bloomstrom of Northlich, for instance, has created a profile for uncovering customers who can influence the purchase decisions of others. (John says that only about 20 percent of the population fits this profile.) In order to make the cut, the individual must have a strong desire to provide helpful advice and they must be able to influence someone else to purchase (by doing things like not selling too hard). His short questionnaire is usually completed online.

Here's an example of how it might work: A female is researching various cosmetic creams on the Internet. At one site, she is offered the opportunity to receive free samples in exchange for filling out a form that asks her a series of questions John has developed. If her answers fit the profile of an advocate, she will continue to receive samples and her opinion may also be solicited. The chief purpose, of course, is to create the goodwill that motivates an advocate to recommend the brand to others.

Now let's explore this application for companies that sell to other businesses.

Turning Customers into the Sales Force

Fortunately, it's a lot simpler in the business-to-business sector to turn customers into the sales force; it's called word of mouth (WOM). Although it has been around a long time, it remains one of the most effective ways of acquiring a customer.

A word-of-mouth referral system can involve one or more of the following types of referrals: professional referrals, professional alliances, customer referrals, advocates, and Industry Influencers. Here is a brief summary of each type of referral.

Professional Referrals

A professional, such as an accountant or an attorney, refers someone to your organization. Many organizations rely almost exclusively on this type of referral.

PROFESSIONAL ALLIANCES

This occurs when three or four businesses refer customers to each other. For instance, five or six consultants may refer each other to their clients.

This is a very effective way to develop business, but it's critical for each consultant to thoroughly understand how the work of each consultant overlaps (for instance, a sales consultant and a marketing consultant). The other "watch out" is that if one consultant does a poor job or is difficult to work with, the client may hold it against the other consultants.

CUSTOMER REFERRALS

This is the easiest type of WOM to control. It simply involves asking the customer to refer you to someone else who has a similar need. Asking for a customer testimonial can also lead to other work, particularly if it is an individual or organization with visibility in the market.

ADVOCATES

Advocates are customers who really like your product and frequently recommend it to other people. (In the consumer space, they are often referred to as "influencers").

INDUSTRY INFLUENCERS

Mention in an article in the *Wall Street Journal* is an example of this type of WOM. You will want to forward any PR like this to your customers. This can help them in the internal selling process.

EMBEDDING OLD WITH NEW

One interesting aspect of these new trends is how traditional marketing methods are either embedded in the new system or used in new ways. For instance, Procter & Gamble found that because teenagers rarely get mail, direct marketing pieces were a great method for providing coupons and product information to advocates.

One of the great hurdles for consumer organizations is effectively managing new mediums for communicating. A business may find it more effective, for instance, to outsource the fulfillment of online requests for samples. However, if their suppliers engage in practices like spamming, this will alienate consumers (which does suggest resisting changing business processes has a rational component).

Chapter 20

End-Of-The-Chapter Questions

1. How could you make your product and your organization even more fun for customers?

2. What events do you (or could you) host to create meaningful learning experiences for employees?

3. What kind of customer experiences could create an ongoing lead system for your organization?

Chapter 21

Answers To Special Challenges

If you only have a few customers, you may have some or all of the following concerns:

> *Is there something about my business that only attracts a small number of customers? How can I make my product attractive to a large number of potential customers? Do my customers represent the thinking of most customers in this market? How do I become the best?*

This chapter will help you answer all of these questions and concerns.

Having A Few Customers Has Some Advantages

Many products and services are created in a vacuum. Once an organization has many customers, delivery becomes so important that it is even more difficult to find the time to step back and look at the business objectively. With only a few customers, you have an opportunity to make some adjustments that may pay real dividends.

COMMON PROBLEMS

Here's a rundown on the common problems small businesses face:

PRODUCT DOESN'T SOLVE A KEY BUSINESS PAIN

In order to create a deep relationship with an organization, your product needs to solve a key business challenge. Not all products have the capacity to do that.

A professional services firm offering training in business etiquette is frequently part of a larger program in a professional development series. This means that selling will require an ongoing promotional effort in order to be there when that type of scenario unfolds.

A more common scenario is that the business has the capacity to solve a key business problem, but the seller is not framing the message in a way that the customer understands.

A BAD BUSINESS MODEL

The best business models create an ongoing stream of revenue. For instance, many chiropractors create this situation by making the case that patients must return regularly to maintain the proper alignment. They may also sell other related products, such as massage therapy, supplements, exercise devices, and specialized pillows.

There are businesses that provide solutions without creating an ongoing stream of revenue. This type of business depends on referrals for survival. For instance, Bill Neff is an expert in using massage to correct alignment problems in the neck and back. If the problem does not require a surgical solution, he works with the patient in three sessions.

If he can't solve the problem, he does not continue the process. Fortunately, Bill solves most problems he sees. This enables him to create an ongoing patient referral base of satisfied clients who recommend him to two or three friends.

In the professional services arena, a marketing firm may provide public relations services on a retainer for a small business. Executives may resist paying for advice, but they are willing to outsource processes that are difficult or costly to staff.

Just A Few Customers

If you don't have a lot of customers, you can learn a great deal by reflecting on the experiences you've had with past customers. In fact, even if you have a lot of customers, this exercise can pay real dividends. There are a couple of reasons this produces different results:

1. Customers are often reluctant to provide honest feedback.

2. You may want to take your business in a new direction.

3. You are usually in the best position to understand the potential of your product.

One way to gain additional insight is to turn each customer situation into a written success story. This will provide you with a great deal of insight into what you actually accomplished and how you might improve.

Also consider what customers wanted and what they might have wanted if you'd had it. For instance, I realized that many of my clients talked about creating a book that highlighted success stories or some other aspect of the business. Consequently, I now offer that as part of my consulting services.

Developing More Business

Here are some concrete steps you can take to understand your market and to develop more business if you don't have a lot of customers.

Elaine Schneider

Conduct A Benchmark Study With Prospects

The purpose of this type of study is to get a much clearer picture of the needs and wants of the C-level executive. It can also lead to an opportunity to develop business. If you don't have a lot of customers, this can be conducted by talking to prospective C-level customers. Several small businesses jump-started their business by doing this.

You might consider hiring a graduate student to make the calls. If you do that, you can include a question asking if the interviewee is looking for help in the areas covered in the survey. This is your opening to hit two birds with one stone by creating a business opportunity.

You are looking for a better idea of the linkage between your offerings and a key organizational challenge. It's difficult to be more specific. You need to identify what you are not clear on and then develop a survey to smoke out what you don't know.

If you can do this in conjunction with a university or an association, executives are more likely to respond. For instance, the editor of a professional trade journal may agree to publish the results. If that angle doesn't work, a business reporter covering this topic may have an interest in publishing the results.

Because the true purpose of this is to learn more (selling is secondary), you might also consider surveying the manager who would likely be responsible for making sure your product produces the desired results. That individual is often in the best position to tell you how your services fit in the context of their business and what they are currently doing (and plan to do in the future).

To get you started in devising the survey, you might consider which market segment or niche does the most work with you and then consider the following questions: What prompted your customers to use you? What pain or pains are you solving with your offerings?

With prospective customers, you will want to know what their key challenges are, what kind of internal resources they are using to address the challenges, and how their approach is working. When prospects evaluate options, they often decide to continue to do it internally or to do nothing.

DETERMINE THE MARKERS OF YOUR IDEAL CUSTOMER

What are the markers that suggest an organization may need your product or service? Knowing this helps you to create a profile of your ideal customer. It is also useful in preparing for an initial meeting with a prospect and it enables you to understand the challenges customers face better than they do.

Here are some of my markers for evaluating a prospective customer: Does the customer's website show a lack of personality? Is the customer in many unrelated markets? Does the customer lack a whole-product solution? Does the customer fail to follow up on brochure requests? Does the customer generate at least $5 million in revenue per year?

You can learn this information by visiting the customer's website, reading recent press releases, talking to the customer's customers and employees, and using databases that provide information on revenue and other indicators. Many libraries provide free online access to these databases.

IMPROVE YOUR METHODOLOGY

A methodology describes your process. You can often create new product attributes around your current products by clarifying your delivery process.

For instance, a group of consultants that sell and install manufacturing systems might realize that an organizational assessment tool might help the customer with issues such as training, quality, and internal communications (and improve acceptance of the new manufacturing system).

I recently worked with a sales consultant who was having difficulty coming up with a tagline and a twenty-second elevator pitch. As we talked, the reason he was having difficulty became clear – he did not have a success story.

In addition to understanding the goals of the key C-level decision maker, he needed to understand the customer's internal barriers to success. This is true in every customer situation. Without an organizational assessment tool as part of his methodology, he was jumping to a training solution without understanding the situation in a larger context.

The fact that he had successful experiences prior to starting his own business suggests that he took right actions in the past because he understood the overall situation. This again illustrates the need for an organizational assessment.

IMPROVE YOUR SELLING PROCESS

As we've already discussed, mapping your sales process will illuminate ways in which you can improve your organization's selling outcomes.

CREATE MORE CREDIBILITY

There are simple, inexpensive ways to create credibility. For instance, a research consultant volunteered to conduct a series of focus groups for members of a local marketing association. Her name and her published conclusions were widely circulated in a monthly newsletter to the five hundred members.

DEVELOP OTHER PRODUCTS AND SERVICES

As you are conducting a phone survey, you might also be looking for opportunities to extend your current offering. Product companies extend their product lines by creating services; service companies create concrete products.

For instance, Pitney Bowes provides financing terms that are below bank rates for their equipment, GE provides airlines with a fleet of technicians who do regular routine maintenance on their airplanes. Technology companies provide service maintenance contracts for repairs and upgrades to their software systems. Service companies create products like training videos and testing materials.

Partner With An Industry Influencer

John Bloomstroom of Northlich shared with me that the Heath Sciences brand of dog food got a huge following by writing a textbook for veterinarian students on animal nutrition. Short of investing this type of time and commitment, there are many things you might consider, such as writing for a local business publication or hosting a monthly speaker series with an association or university.

Any activity that creates more visibility also inspires you to stay informed about your industry. Internationally respected speaker Brian Tracy recommends reading one hour per day in your area of expertise.

Create an Advisory Board

Paul Slaggert, the former director of a management development center at the University of Cincinnati, was losing money on his public seminar series. He came up with the idea of selling a certain number of seats to large Fortune 500 and Fortune 1000 companies in the region. He reasoned that these organizations were each spending a great deal of money to develop content that could be shared across a number of companies at a significant cost saving. He created an advisory board of human resource executives to identify common needs.

It took almost a year to develop the program, but Paul believes the results were worth it. Once it was in place, his center received a large lump sum from the region's largest corporations to finance the entire year at a reasonable profit. In addition, he eliminated the unpredictable risk that public seminars create.

Paul said the biggest challenge was to resist the temptation to impose his ideas on the group in the early phases. He wanted to avoid ending up with his version of a virtual corporate university program.

Final Thought

None of these activities will automatically bring business to your door. It will take time. An event, for instance, allows you to collect business cards in exchange for the opportunity to win a gift. This creates a database for sending a newsletter or using some other mechanism for keeping you in front of potential customers.

Chapter 21

End-Of-The-Chapter Questions

1. Did you find one or two useful ideas in this chapter? If so, what were the ideas?

2. Do you participate in a roundtable with a group of small-business owners? If not, are there other activities that help you gain perspective on your business and manage your attitude?

Chapter 22

Finding The Right Marketing Resources

As your business continues to grow, you will want to find someone who can support your efforts in developing and maintaining the optimal marketing infrastructure. This chapter will focus on the individual who fits the ideal profile for this task.

Small businesses are wise to hire a consultant or—if they can do it financially—an individual with marketing expertise as soon as it is feasible. A small business needs a marketing generalist who has an in-depth background in sales and marketing.

Someone who can wear both hats has the highest probability of being successful in creating a marketing infrastructure. This is because selling teaches you how to execute. An individual who comes from a sales background is more likely to be able to implement a strategy, unlock the ideal customer profile and communicate the value of the product.

Ideally, you also want someone who has experience in your industry. Research shows that individuals with at least five years of experience in an industry are most likely to succeed when starting their own businesses.

THE RIGHT PERSONALITY

Because customer dialogues are the linchpin of creating and maintaining a marketing infrastructure, it is critical to find someone who is able to establish rapport within the first critical minutes of a phone conversation with a C-level executive. The planned questions are not as critical as the follow-up questions.

CNN talk show host Larry King asks what probably are the best types of nonthreatening questions. Of course, his approach must be adjusted to a business setting. Being able to convert raw data from customers into insight and patterns is also critical. This can not be emphasized enough.

I came to realize this while listening to a tape called *Now Discover Your Strengths*.[18] The marketing generalist you select must be able to network, discern patterns in the information he or she is getting from customers, and sell.

PERSONALITY PROFILE

The key elements consist of:

1. Being able to pick up the phone and immediately engage the person on the other end of the phone (skills of networking).

2. Having high business literacy. This entails absorbing what is being said and developing cogent follow-up questions (insight).

3. Knowing when to go for the jugular (skills of selling) by picking the right moment to suggest how your organization may be able to help a customer with a key challenge.

CONTENT KNOWLEDGE

At a minimum, content knowledge entails:

1. Knowledge of how to create a marketing infrastructure.

2. A sales process (and a track record of selling). I like *Solution Selling* for managing the face-to-face part of selling and *Strategic Selling* for managing the various Buying Influences in a sale.

3. Influence skills. One key element is being receptive to other perspectives and leveraging the ideas of others.

4. Facilitation skills. A structured facilitation process is essential for sharing customer data. It is often done in the context of solving a burning marketing issue.

5. Proactive Gene. An ability to consistently uncover a variety of ways to sell and innovate. This includes things like developing a few back-of-the-envelope numbers for running the business.

SALARY STRUCTURE

One of the reasons hiring a salesperson is so attractive is the commission-based structure. Hiring someone to do a mix of sales and marketing clearly requires either a salary structure or a mix of salary and commission structures. Another option is to offer a percentage of future revenue.

Hiring a marketing consultant enables you to offer a more flexible salary arrangement and to test the impact on your business. For instance, rainmakers thrive in the current system and can sabotage efforts to move from a sales-driven organization to a marketing-driven organization.

The right marketing consultant can also engage other people in the organization in thinking in new ways about developing more business from current customers. This includes areas such as customer service, sales, and technical support.

EXECUTION OF A MARKETING INFRASTRUCTURE

The first few months of working with a marketing generalist are critical. This is because he or she is in the best position to help you get a clear perspective on your challenges and the barriers to even better performance.

This clarity will diminish over time. As the generalist works with your organization, he or she will unconsciously learn to work within the constraints of your organization.

For instance, the leader of a consulting firm that generates about $3 million in sales complains that the business is not very profitable. She further acknowledges that the staff is highly disorganized.

It quickly becomes clear that the firm has four different consulting services without a common business process. No wonder the staff is disorganized and the firm is not very profitable. In addition, the two partners keep the staff in the dark about the status of their accounts, but blame individual staff members when there is a snafu that results in a customer service problem. The lack of product synergy also means that the cost of managing internal operations is too high.

First One Hundred Days

The first one hundred days are the most critical in establishing priorities. The first order of business is to describe three things: the key challenge, the internal barriers and the existing marketing infrastructure. Internal barriers are really disconnects between stated goals and actions.

Every organization is different. The process described below provides a general framework. You will have additional questions and you may add other elements to each phase.

Phase 1: Initial Organizational Assessment

1. Identify the key challenge. Scenerio: A client is in eight markets. Its products are becoming more difficult to sell.

2. Establish who is the sponsor (ideally the most senior person).

3. Translate goals into action. Scenario: A client wishes to make $1 million per year in his consulting business, but his client list consists of other small businesses.

4. Identify internal barriers. Scenario: A consulting firm wants to work with privately-held businesses. Prospective customers have consistently told the executive director she needs to develop a success story.

5. Assess the current level of a marketing infrastructure. There are four likely scenarios listed:
    Level 1: No process for a continuous dialogue with customers.
    Level 2: Some communication processes, little understanding of customers' pains, inconsistent sales funnel, sell in six unrelated markets.
    Level 3: All the elements of a marketing infrastructure are in place, but not enough time is spent on a key element (such as working with Industry Influencers).
    Level 4: All the elements of a marketing infrastructure are in place. The business wants to uncover a new, related market.

6. Revisit initial description of challenge. Scenario: Our current products are not selling. We need to eliminate what is not selling and find a niche market that will lead us to new product offerings.

PHASE 2: ANALYSIS (INITIAL SAMPLE QUESTIONS)

1. What information is needed from the customer?

2. Which customers (or other stakeholders) can be useful?

3. How can we involve these customers (or other stakeholders) in addressing our challenge?

PHASE 3: IMPLEMENTATION

1. Review customer surveys with the leadership team. Begin to review specific opportunties that will address the key challenge.

2. Based on feedback, outline an action plan for addressing internal barriers and developing a product feasibility study, if appropriate.

3. Review current product and service offerings. Are there products or services that are not producing results or require a great deal of overhead? Develop criteria for evaluating what stays; what goes.

4. Address the marketing infrastructure. If weak or missing elements of the marketing infrastructure exist, how can it be improved? Outline an action plan for addressing specific weaknesses.

5. Integrate all the pieces into a master plan with specific time lines (this will serve as the framework for a marketing plan).

6. Improve (if needed) front office processes, such sales funnel management and customer database maintenance. Review communications such as Internet, etc.

7. Set up an ongoing review process. Modify the master plan as needed.

Chapter 22

End-Of-The-Chapter Questions

1. What other abilities or specialized knowledge does a marketing generalist need in your market?

2. What key insights did you gain from the book?

3. Are there things you could do immediately to generate new business? Make a list of action plans you will institute to support the profitable growth of your business.

Chapter 23

Creating The Results You Want

In an earlier part of the book, Laurie Althaus was quoted as saying that small-business owners need to work *on* the business, not just *in* the business. The implication is that if business owners bring a higher level of consciousness to the daily activities of the business, they will realize better results. However, right actions will not provide all you want and deserve. You must also be able to create the outcomes you desire.

> *To create what you want, you must devote time each day to practices that enable you to construct the future you want. This is the subject of the final chapter.*

Putting It All Together

So far, we've spent a great deal of time focusing on the structures you can create to help you work smart. This includes developing a marketing infrastructure to create a laser focus, using operating principles to streamline the management of your business, and adopting new marketing trends in order to engage customers and employees at a deeper level (and ultimately sell more).

Developing the right business structures is important. Here is why. Each element of a marketing infrastructure has a complimentary relationship. This enables you to get a flywheel effect. For instance, there is a dynamic connection between developing dialogues with customers and uncovering a niche market. Customers illuminate new opportunties. Similarly, synergy exists between each of the operating principles. For example, creating a value proposition with all the stakeholders in your organization makes it easier to manage scarce resources wisely. By providing the right things in the first place, it's easier to see where resources need to be allocated.

As a bonus, the operating principles support (and are consistent with) the elements of a marketing infrastructure. These two constructs—a marketing infrastructure and operating principles—are also consistent with new trends in marketing. This is because the overall objective of the new trends is to forge a deeper relationship with the customer in order to create products customers want. The overall effect is better results with fewer resources.

However, as just alluded to at the beginning of the chapter, self-management is another critical dimension of creating the outcomes you want. We all know individuals who are able to consistently get the results they want. In many cases, it is not because they are smarter.

Why Some People Are Stellar Performers

They possess a secret that enables them to operate at a higher level. What sets them apart is their ability to visualize in very concrete ways, the things they want to create. They can actually see (and feel) themselves succeeding in whatever they want to achieve. Actor Will Smith, whose movies have grossed more than $400 million in the USA alone, speaks to this effect when he says, "I have no doubts at all. There is power in believing something that manifests itself in reality."

A Mind Left To Its Own Devices

Unfortunately, negative thoughts can also be powerful. A few years ago, I began to have a premonition that a small child would run between two parked cars as I was driving down the street. This picture would pop into my mind from time to time. I couldn't seem to shake it. I avoided side streets whenever possible.

About a year after I began having these premonitions, I was driving down the side street next to my house when a child ran out between two cars. Fortunately, I was able to stop in time.

Positive Manifestations

Early in my career, I sensed that my position in sales would lead to some sort of opportunity in the field of training (an area of keen interest to me). Because I was unfamiliar with the concept of bringing ideas into reality, this remained a vague concept for several years. For this reason, I believe it took longer to happen.

In fact, I almost missed the article about a university-based management development consulting group that wanted to open doors into the business community. Although I had no experience in the training field, I realized my background in sales would be helpful in opening doors. I was hired first as a consultant and then as a director.

Bringing To Life What You Are Thinking

What's behind these stories? A new set of scientific knowledge that is referred to as Chaos Theory sheds some light on this. I will spare you all the scientific details (of which you may already be aware) and simply state that there is evidence that suggests we attract the things we are thinking into our lives.

In addition to a growing number of scientists who can cite scientific evidence to support this contention, well-respected best-selling authors like Depak Chopra and Wayne Dyer contend you can attract into your life the people and events that will be instrumental in creating the outcomes you desire.

Best-selling author Robert Fritz also references this in his book *Your Life As Art*. He says, "...another thing happens that is hard to explain.

There is almost a mystical dimension. Coincidences begin to occur regularly." [19]

If you find this way of thinking hard to swallow, I don't believe it is critical that you believe that the right people will appear or that you can manifest whatever you want to create. The fact is that if you switch from thinking in terms of getting rid of something to thinking in terms of creating what you want in your life, you immediately begin to take actions that reinforce what you want.

Why Getting Rid Of Something Doesn't Work

Bill was looking for a job, but he was convinced he was too old to be hired. All of his behaviors were focused on getting rid of something—unemployment. He had a negative vibe. This further frustrated any attempt he made to attract what he wanted into his life. He had, in effect, created a shield that stopped anything positive from entering his life.

If Bill continues to be convinced that none of his actions will bring him closer to his objective, he will unconsciously sabotage opportunities that contradict the story he has created.

On the other hand, if Bill faced the brutal fact that his age could be a liability, he could turn it into an advantage much like some eastern forms of fighting teach you to move toward the aggressor in order to leverage the opponent's strength. Notice that this is not magical thinking. In fact, part of the creative process is facing the brutal facts of your situation.

If you have read the book *Good to Great*, you may recall that Jim Collins puts a great deal of emphasis on the fact that facing the brutal facts is a key success factor for those organizations on his short list of good to great companies. [20] You may also recall my observation that the key to a breakthrough is often the moment a business recognizes what it doesn't do well.

How Creating Changes The Dynamics

Bill might turn a perceived liability (age) into an asset (experience) by creating "products" that reflect his interests and knowledge. As part of his job hunt, he might develop a website consisting of a virtual interview. This would give him an opportunity to showcase his accomplishments.

Individuals who are innately creative (or those who understand the creative process) seem to follow a similar process. The first step is to spend time every day visualizing what you want to create. If you're an artist, you might do some sketches before attempting to commit what you wish to create on canvas.

If you are creating a new business, you might cut out pictures and paste them onto a storyboard to describe what you will be doing. The objective is to make it as concrete as possible. You can see how this activity enables you to begin to see a way forward.

However, in the early stages, it is not important to know how you will actually accomplish what you want to do. The *how* will come later. In the beginning, you want to make it so real that you can feel what it is you'd like to have.

Being grateful seems to be another important component. I know of one senior-level executive who constantly communicated how lucky he was even when things seemed to be taking a disastrous turn. Recently he was tapped for the top position in a $200 million company despite losing over $60 million in an ill-conceived venture.

The Magic Of Daily Practices

Probably the most important advice is to develop daily practices that enable you to gain perspective and go deeper. These practices help you to create a higher level of consciousness (which reduces mindless activity and supports actions that get results). Some ways to do this include meditating, exercising, and keeping a daily journal. The goal is to be less outwardly directed and more inwardly directed.

It's important not to get too caught up in the daily news. News is designed to create fear and hopelessness. You can't create what you want in your life if you are feeling that things are beyond your control. Instead, make time each day—even if it's just a few minutes—to read inspirational books. This provides a sense of hopefulness. There are many books on tape you can listen to while you are driving. Music also elevates mood and stimulates creativity.

Simple Ways To Bring Creativity To Life

If you would like to bring more creativity to your life, start with a small project that you enjoy doing. It does not have to be a work-related project. In fact, you might stimulate more creativity by doing something you enjoy that involves working with your hands. This can be something as simple as planting a garden or painting a garage. Notice the sense of satisfaction you have from doing these projects.

If this approach does not work, you might try organizing your space in ways that free up your creativity or you may simply eliminate all the clutter that gets in your way.

One entrepreneur was in three different businesses. This left her feeling like she could never really get any traction. Feeling frustrated by her own lack of organization, she straightened up her desk and cleaned her office. Six weeks later, she found a way to integrate the three businesses under one banner. Within a year, she was successful in doubling her business. She credits decluttering with creating the space for new ideas.

The more you can actually see and feel yourself accomplishing your objective, the more concrete and doable it will become. Sometimes it helps to imagine what you will be wearing or to visualize what a day in your life will be like when you are doing all the things you want to do in your life.

Balancing Planning and Experimentation

After you have spent time visualizing what you want to create, you will be ready to develop an overall objective. The objective should include a detailed description of exactly what you want to accomplish. Next you need to include the specific tactics you will employ to accomplish the objective.

This, of course, will change as you experiment with the various action plans you outlined. Learning from trial and error is critical. Recognizing what is not working is part of the creative process.

The important thing is to keep your vision of what you want to accomplish before you every day. This enables you to also monitor how well you are doing in reaching your goal.

To Summarize...

To work *on* the business not just *in* the business requires the discipline of a process. It starts by understanding that you must face the brutal facts of your business so that you can take right actions.

Secondly, you must develop a marketing infrastructure and a set of organizing principles that enable you to leverage your time and energy (and spend more time experimenting with newer marketing trends). Finally, self-discipline enables you to bring a higher level of consciousness to your work, which in turn enables you to create the outcomes you want in your life. If you are already able to create what you want, you know the power of this freedom.

REFERENCE NOTES

1. Drucker, Peter with Joseph A. Maciariello. *The Daily Drucker; 366 Days Of Insight And Motivation For Getting The Right Things Done.* New York: Harper Business, 2004.
2. Beckwith, Harry. *The Invisible Touch. The Four Keys To Modern Marketing.* New York: Warner Books, 2000.
3. McKenna, Regis. *Relationship Marketing. Successful Strategies for the Age of the Customer.* Boston: Addison-Wesley, 1991.
4. Fritz, Robert. *Your Life As Art.* Vermont: Newfane Press, 2004.
5. Bonoma, Thomas V. *The Marketing Edge: Making Strategies Work.* New York: Free Press, 1985.
6. Miller, Robert B, Heiman, Stephen E. and Tuleja Tad. *Strategic Selling: The Unique Sales System Proven Successful by America's Best Companies.* New York: W. Morrow, 1985.
7. Collins, Jim. *Good to Great: Why Some Companies Make the Leap...and Others Don't.* New York: HarperCollins, 2002.
8. Levitt, Theodore. *The Marketing Imagination.* New York: Free Press, 1983.
9. Kotler, Philip. *Kotler on Marketing: How To Create, Win and Dominate Markets.* New York: Free Press, 1985.
10. Levitt, Theodore. *The Marketing Imagination.* New York: Free Press, 1983.
11. Cooper, Robert G. *Winning At New Products: Accelerating The Process From Idea To Launch.* Cambridge, Massachusetts: Perseus Publishing, 2001.
12. Levitt, Theodore. *The Marketing Imagination.* New York: Free Press, 1983.
13. Quinlan, Mary Lou. *Just Ask A Woman: Cracking The Code of What Woman Want And How They Buy.* Hoboken, New Jersey: J. Wiley & Sons, 2003.
14. Bonoma, Thomas V. *The Marketing Edge: Making Strategies Work.* New York: Free Press, 1985.
15. Bonoma, Thomas V. *The Marketing Edge: Making Strategies Work.* New York: Free Press, 1985.

16. Sutton, Robert I. *Weird Ideas That Work: 11½ Practices for Promoting, Managing, and Sustaining Innovation.* New York: The Free Press, 2002.
17. Pine II, B. Joseph, Gilmore, James H.. *The Experience Economy: Work is Theater and Every Business a Stage.* Boston: Harvard Business School Press, 1999.
18. Buckingham, Marcus, Clifton, Donald O. *Now Discover Your Strengths.* New York: Free Press, 2001.
19. Fritz, Robert, *Your Life As Art.* Vermont: Newfane Press, 2004.
20. Collins, Jim. *Good to Great: Why Some Companies Make the Leap… and Others Don't.* New York: HarperCollins, 2002.

Bellman, Geoffrey M. *The Consultant's Calling: Bringing Who You Are To What You Do.* San Francisco: Jossey-Bass Inc., 1990.
Beckwith, Harry. *Selling The Invisible: A Field Guide To Modern Marketing.* New York: Warner Books, 1997.
Beckwith, Harry. *The Invisible Touch. The Four Keys To Modern Marketing.* New York: Warner Books, 2000.
Bonoma, Thomas V. *The Marketing Edge: Making Strategies Work.* New York: Free Press, 1985.
Bosworth, Michael T. *Solution Selling: Creating Buyers in Difficult Selling Markets.* New York: McGraw Hill, 1995.
Collins, Jim. *Good to Great: Why Some Companies Make the Leap…and Others Don't.* New York: HarperCollins, 2002.
Cooper, Robert G. *Winning At New Products: Accelerating The Process From Idea To Launch.* Cambridge, Massachusetts: Perseus Publishing, 2001.
Drucker, Peter. *The Daily Drucker; 366 Days Of Insight And Motivation For Getting The Right Things Done.* New York: Harper Business, 2004.
Edwards, Sarah, Edwards, Paul. *Making It On Your Own: Learning And Thriving On The Ups And Downs of Being Your Own Boss.* New York: St. Martin's Press, 1991.
Edwards, Sarah, Edwards, Paul *Getting Business to Come to You: Everything You Need To Do Your Own Advertising, Public Relations, Direct Mail and Sales Promotion And Attract All The Business You Can Handle.* Los Angles: J.P. Torcher, 1991.
Fritz, Robert. *Your Life as Art.* Vermont: Newfane Press, 2004.

Fritz, Robert. *Path of Least Resistance: Learning To Become The Creative Force in Your Own Life.* New York: Ballantine, 1989.

Hamel, Gary, Prahalad C.K. *Competing For The Future.* Boston: Harvard Business School Press, 1994.

Handy, Charles. *The Elephant and the Flea: Reflections of a Reluctant Capitalist.* Boston: Harvard Business School Press, 2001.

Kelly, Tom. *The Art of Innovation.* New York: Doubleday, 2001.

Kotler, Philip, Hayes, Thomas J and Bloom, Paul N. *Marketing Professional Services: Forward Thinking Strategies For Boosting Your Business, Your Image And Your Profits.* Paramus, New Jersey: Prentice Hall, 2002.

Kotler, Philip. *Kotler on Marketing: How To Create, Win and Dominate Markets.* New York: Free Press, 1985.

Loehr, Jim, Schwartz,Tony. *The Power of Full Engagement, Managing Energy, Not Time, Is The Key To High Performance and Personal Renewal.* New York: Free Press, 2003.

Levinson, Jay Conrad. *Guerrilla Marketing Attack: New Strategies, Tactics & Weapons for Winning Big Profits From Your Small Business.* Boston: Houghton Mifflin Company, 1989.

Levitt, Theodore. *The Marketing Imagination.* New York: Free Press, 1983.

McKenna, Regis. *Relationship Marketing. Successful Strategies for the Age of the Customer.* Boston: Addison-Wesley, 1991.

Miller, Robert B, Heiman, Stephen E. and Tuleja Tad. *Strategic Selling: The Unique Sales System Proven Successful by America's Best Companies.* New York: W. Morrow, 1985.

Moore, Geoffrey A. *Crossing the Chasm: Marketing & Selling High Tech Products to Mainstream Customers.* New York: Harper Business, 1999.

Moore, Geoffrey A. *Inside The Tornado: Marketing Strategies From Silicon Valley's Cutting Edge.* New York: Harper Business, 1995.

Peppers, Don and Martha Rogers. *The One to One Future: Building Relationships One Customer at a Time.* New York: Doubleday, 1993.

Pine II, Joseph, Gilmore, James B.. *The Experience Economy: Work is Theater and Every Business a Stage.* Boston: Harvard Business School Press, 1999.

Quinlan, Mary Lou. *Just Ask A Woman: Cracking The Code of What Woman Want And How They Buy.* Hoboken, New Jersey: J. Wiley & Sons, 2003.

Rackham, Neil. *Spin Selling.* New York: McGraw Hill, 1988.
Sabath, Ann Marie. *Courting Business: 101 Ways for Accelerating Business Relationships.* New Jersey: Career Press, 2005.
Senge, Peter. *The Fifth Discipline: The Art and Practice of the Learning Organization.* New York: Doubleday, 1990.
Sutton, Robert I. *Weird Ideas That Work: 111/2 Practices for Promoting, Managing, and Sustaining Innovation.* New York: The Free Press, 2002.
Wheatly, Margaret J. *Leadership And The New Science. Discovering Order In A New World.* San Francisco: Berrett-Koehler, 2006.
Zyman, Sergio, *The End of Marketing As We Know It.* Hoboken, New Jersey: John Wiley & Sons, 2002.

Appendix

A Guide To Event Planning
Appendix I, II

Creating a customer experience is a great platform for showcasing your capabilities. Appendix l and ll provides a ready reference if you are considering either a proprietary event or a trade show.

The section on proprietary events will also help you if you are making a presentation. (See the heading labeled "Content Presentation."). It provides useful advice on framing your message and managing the audience.

Like any execution activity, an event needs to be carefully planned. Poorly planned events produce few tangible results and can actually create adverse consequences. For example, if you allow uninvited guests to participate they may use the event to sell their products. This will virtually guarantee that many participants will not show up for future events.

It might surprise you to know that, occasionally, a trade show can actually be the best way to promote an intangible service. This proves there are never any hard and fast rules in marketing.

You will also find that many of the preparations for a trade show are applicable to other events. For instance, taking the time and effort to plan how members of your organization can actively engage participants. The tips may be obvious, but can be overlooked during the planning process.

Appendix I

Events

A proprietary event is a platform. It is used to showcase your capabilities and to foster a dialogue.

Types of Proprietary Events

Proprietary events include the following types of formats: panel of experts, focus groups, executive briefings, roundtables, user groups, seminars, conferences, speakers' bureaus, and advisory boards, to name a few.

Proprietary Event Basics

Each event format accomplishes slightly different outcomes. A seminar can be a great business development tool, but a focus group is generally not a good vehicle for developing business. (In the last heading, "The Science of Selecting Formats," we will cover this in more detail).

The Angle

The content can accomplish one of three things: provide a crystal ball into the future, explore some challenge in the participant's industry, or provide information that the participant can use to immediately be more effective.

Any business that is able to solve a key pain in a customer's organization is in the best position to hold an event that will attract C-level participants (because you are dealing with issues they care about).

The Keys To Effective Events

There are three things most organizations fail to do. They are the most critical elements of developing an event designed to generate business.

They are: get the key decision maker into the room, get participants to talk, and follow up with participants.

Typical Outcomes Of An Event

An event can create many of the same outcomes that a phone survey creates, but an event is clearly a better vehicle for educating customers and prospects on your capabilities and creating emotional commitment. Typical outcomes include:

1. Adding to the top of the sales funnel and moving potential sales to the end of the sales funnel.

2. Turning customers into advocates (asking them to be on a panel is a good method for doing this).

3. Increasing credibility.

Web-Based Presentations

If you have a geographically dispersed customer base, it's tempting to hold a web-based proprietary event. Companies like Web Ex can show you how to create a seminar that doesn't have the look and feel of a product pitch, but it's not the same thing as a holding an event in a room filled with people.

In person, events provide opportunities for participants to network and interact with each other. You also have an opportunity to have conversations with customers and prospects that simply cannot be duplicated by technology.

Events Gone Awry

A speaker at an American Marketing Association event made a brief, self-serving remark at the beginning of his presentation. A number of members were upset. At another event, five executives sent people who report to them. In both instances, the host organization was undone within the first few minutes.

Had the speaker understood that if you give knowledge away you generate emotional commitment, he would have avoided the self-serving remark. Had the second organization framed the event as being invitation-only, the second problem would have been avoided.

EXECUTION: THE SIX STEPS TO A SUCCESSFUL EVENT

There are six steps to a successful event. They are: logistics, objective setting, targeted audience development, content presentation, follow up, and measurement.

LOGISTICS

Simplicity is the key. Logistics is a critical element, but has nothing to do with business results. A simple early morning breakfast is inexpensive and effective.

OBJECTIVE SETTING

The sign of a well-conceived marketing activity is one that accomplishes multiple objectives. For instance, your objectives for an event may be three-fold: to develop five new business opportunities, to move the sales process to a conclusion with three prospects, and to promote an ongoing roundtable series.

TARGETED AUDIENCE DEVELOPMENT

It is critical to uncover the key decision maker for your product when developing an invitation list for an event. A good rule of thumb is to identify who you believe that person is and then invite that person's boss. The boss is probably the actual decision maker. If you're dealing with a prospect, you can figure out who the key decision maker is with some detective work. This includes tools such as business databases, surveys, and referrals.

CONTENT PRESENTATION

It's important to get information about your audience before creating the content. If possible, you will want to talk to several customers or Industry Influencers to help you frame the topic and content.

Consider your audience very carefully before you go beyond the basics. I learned this the hard way. I recall giving a presentation on the topic of marketing to a group of government scientists. I knew they were very smart, so I assumed they would appreciate a program that went beyond the basics of marketing. I was wrong. On the other hand, I did a very basic presentation on doing a needs assessment to a group of consultants and they loved it.

> *Always start with some basic frame of reference so that everyone is operating off of the same basic mental model (even if they are experts). I learned another important corollary fact. Unless someone has had exactly the same experience you have, don't expect that person to know what you know.*

Over and over again, I observe people thinking someone is incompetent because they think if they know something, everyone else should know what they know. This same thinking occurs when making presentations.

Speakers who have too much content seem to do it to avoid questions they may not be able to answer. If you are concerned that you don't have total mastery of the material, do this: Develop content at the highest scale possible (You can do this without being confusing if you keep it simple). This avoids having to know a lot of details. It also makes it more difficult for the audience to formulate questions you may not be able to answer.

When creating content, you must decide how you want to approach your audience. I think it's always safer to confidently present information, but be open to the input of the audience. Another tactic is to clarify your expertise. For instance, a human resource consultant said that he could not answer questions regarding the financial section of a presentation involving several speakers. When you are up-front and open, you avoid the potential to look foolish.

The key is to get the audience involved early so that you can deflect a tough question by asking someone from the audience to comment. For instance, you may introduce some distinguished members of the audience or a group from the same organization. If you are doing a panel discussion, the moderator may ask the audience if they have questions or comments when the opportunity presents itself. This is particularly important when conducting a panel or a roundtable because you can't map out exactly what will transpire.

A few years ago, I attended an American Marketing Association panel discussion on marketing local sporting events. Somewhere in the middle of the discussion, it became clear that everyone on the panel was trying to attract the same demographic. Members of the audience later observed this privately to each other.

Had the moderator been effective in engaging the audience, someone might have directed this observation to the panel and the moderator might have artfully gotten the audience involved (After all, this was a room full of marketers). But then again, saying "Let's stop for a moment and see if the audience has any observations" only works if you have encouraged their participation from the beginning. Instead, the panel lost credibility because the moderator did no address this issue.

A second reason for making an effort to engage the audience is that baby boomers like to hear from each other (I think it's due to a fundamental distrust of authority figures. Remember the mantra "Don't trust anyone over thirty"?)

Participants will frequently value the thoughts of their colleagues more than those of the expert. It's not because they know more than the expert. Quite the opposite—it's because they are experiencing the same challenges and pains. If you don't give participants some air time, they are less likely to like you or the presentation. Again, the end game is creating an emotional commitment.

Follow Up

The lack of a follow-up plan is the fatal flaw in most programs. If an organization needs what you offer, it will be the last to call, but it will also be the most receptive to your call. The reason is simple—there is a natural tendency to procrastinate anything that is necessary but painful. It is simply human nature. The contact can come from marketing or sales. If you or another executive have a deep personal relationship with the participant, perhaps a personal call from you is appropriate.

Here's a story that makes the case for follow-up: After hosting several executive briefings, I planned to contact every participant to get his or her impression of the event. The executive who made the presentations insisted on making the call. I knew he was too busy to make the time to do it. About a week later, one of the participants called. He was clearly upset that I had not called him as a follow-up to the event. At the time, I served on one of the boards he managed, so I was quite surprised that this normally mild-mannered individual was so troubled that he had not been contacted. Upon reflection, I believe he may have concluded from our lack of follow-up that we were not interested in working with him.

Measurement

Events are easy to track. In my experience, events create the kind of credibility that enables you to reduce the sales cycle and improve the close rate by as much as half in the professional services category.

Products or services that require the buyer to change or eliminate an existing business process do not have the same dramatic reduction in the sales cycle, but events would certainly create the circumstances for improving the close rate. The same is true of any product or service that involves a substantial investment.

The Science of Selecting Formats

Each format is superior in achieving certain objectives. For example, seminars can be used to deepen relationships, but they don't work as well as the roundtable format for that purpose.

Linking Objectives To A Format

The chart indicates the format, or formats, that work best with each type of objective listed.

Seminar: **S**
Roundtable **RT**
Focus Group **FG**
Conference **C**

Objective	S	RT	FG	C
Promotion	x			x
New Business	x	x		x
New Product Rollout	x		x	
Relationship Building		x		x
Customer Politics	x			x

Distinctions Between Formats

Here is a brief rundown on the four formats:

1. Seminars and conferences are easy to promote because everyone understands what they are. Both formats are also superior for understanding the politics of a customer's organization.

2. Roundtables and focus groups can be confusing to the public. Roundtables provide a superior format for relationship building because they enable you to explore topics at a deeper level.

However, the more formal nature of the roundtable format may limit how much participants share regarding the politics of their organization.

3. Focus groups are a great way to introduce a product (although it is usually just one aspect of a promotional strategy). Attempting to develop new business using the focus group format will backfire.

4. Conferences offer the most flexibility because other formats can be embedded within them. Conferences are a great way to showcase your organization to Industry Influencers.

Unhappy Customers

You must deal with unhappy customers before the event. Otherwise, you run the risk that they may complain to others. Of course, it is impossible to know for sure what a customer will say to other attendees.

Asking customers to make a presentation is a control factor because this requires them to signal a commitment. You also have the opportunity to work closely with them in the content development phase.

In short, creating customer experiences is an important dimension of creating emotional commitment (and can be an opportunity to deal with unhappy customers). It's important to understand the strengths and the weaknesses of each format. More importantly, a low-cost event can often achieve as much as—or more —than events that are expensive and complex to run. The key is planning.

Appendix II

Trade Shows

Creating customer experiences can involve a number of formats such as trade shows, proprietary events, and user groups. A trade show requires a demonstration. As a result, it has more limitations as a venue for selling a service.

Having said that, there are never any hard and fast rules in marketing. A trade show can sometimes be the most appropriate approach when selling an intangible product.

There are four main purposes of a trade show. They are: identify new customers, develop a database of prospects, reconnect with customers and Industry Influencers, and learn more about the competition.

Trade Show Basics

Trade shows can be a very effective tool if you have a product. For instance, the entry point for selling the Mechanical Dynamics line of software products in the auto industry is engineers. A trade show environment is ideal because it attracts this type of buyer.

Services are usually inappropriate, but not always. LegalEase Solutions LLC does quality, low-cost, routine legal work by outsourcing it to India. It did well at an American Bar Association trade show. Here are some of the reasons why:

1. The theme of the trade show was about new trends in the practice of law.

2. The entire show consisted of decision makers for the company's service.

3. The company made its service tangible by showing a graph of their methodology for managing a legal document.

The main reason LegalEase Solutions resorted to a trade show had to do with the nature of a law practice. Lawyers are too busy reacting to opposing counsel and the demands of their clients to engage in a discussion about their business at work.

While it's true that LegalEase Solutions will have opportunities to make presentations to local legal associations, those take time to develop, and many attorneys who fit the ideal prospect profile don't have time to participate in that type of activity.

Strategic Considerations

Here are some of the considerations if you are evaluating the value of participating in a trade show:

1. Is it the best venue for developing business?

2. Will the decision maker show up?

3. Is this a "must-be-there" trade show?

Although the main motivation was an opportunity to get face time with attorneys, LegalEase Solutions also wanted to assess how receptive attorneys were to the idea of outsourcing routine legal work to India.

As a marketing research tool, it was not a perfect reflection of all attorneys (because those attending wanted to learn about time-saving technologies). On the other hand, this made it the perfect venue for developing a database of contacts predisposed to the company's solution.

Sample Trade Show Outcomes

By talking to a wide variety of attorneys who visited the booth, LegalEase Solutions accomplished six things. They were:

1. Identified prospects
2. Confirmed acceptance of legal outsourcing
3. Improved communication of their story
4. Enhanced their understanding of the application to small law firms
5. Built a newsletter database
6. Scoped out the competition

Planning For A Trade Show

Jim Savage of Savage Marketing Company begins working with an organization about sixteen weeks before the trade show.

Here are some keys to making the trade show productive:

1. Identify goals; measure results.
2. Develop events and programs to complement the trade show.
3. Identify ways you will use the database of contacts from the show.

Working The Booth

Jim starts by helping a client figure out what kind of questions they plan to ask. The right question can be effective in engaging a prospect and setting the tone for the conversation.

The proprietor of an antique shop pointed this out to me when she observed that most retail establishments ask customers if they need help. Instead of doing that, she asks her clientele what they are looking for as soon as they walk in the door. This question produces much better responses.

Jim works with every employee who will be working the booth. Even salespeople must learn how to manage the sales process in a trade show environment. For example, Jim suggests getting rid of tire kickers by leading them away from the booth while talking to them and then quickly concluding the conversation by shaking their hand and thanking them for their time.

Jim also provides simple tools, such as prioritizing prospective customers on a one to three scale and writing notes on the back of the prospect's business card to help with recalling the discussion (this is also an excellent technique when at a networking event).

CREATING VALUE-ADDED TRADE SHOW ACTIVITIES

Additional activities will help your organization get more value from the trade show experience. The activities you select must be consistent with your strengths.

Possibilities include holding a press conference, hosting a panel discussion of Industry Influencers, and inviting customers to attend a focus group. You will, of course, also want to check out your competitors. Value-added activities, such as conducting a focus group, can also be included when hosting a conference.

ABOUT THE AUTHOR

Elaine Schneider has in-depth experience in sales, marketing and organizational development. As a marketing consultant, she specializes in helping organizations with marketing challenges in the professional services sector.

Prior to starting her own business, she was a director at the Center for Management at Xavier University. Other leadership roles include President of the American Marketing Association in Cincinnati and Adjunct Professor in Marketing at Union Institute & University. She received her MBA from Xavier University.

To learn more visit www.elaineschneider.net

Printed in the United States
87704LV00003B/208-225/A